*Mercier Press is the oldest independent Irish
publishing house and has published books in the
fields of history, literature, folklore, music, art,
humour, drama, politics, current affairs, law
and religion. It was founded in 1944 by John
and Mary Feehan.*

*In the building up of a country
few needs are as great as that of a publishing
house which would make the people proud of
their past, and proud of themselves as a people
capable of inspiring and supporting a world of
books which was their very own. Mercier Press
has tried to be that publishing house. On the
occasion of our fiftieth anniversary we thank
the many writers and readers who have
supported us and contributed to our success.*

*We face our second half-century
with confidence.*

IRISH ANIMAL TALES

MICHAEL SCOTT

ILLUSTRATED BY
JOSEPH GERVIN

MERCIER PRESS

Mercier Press
PO Box 5, 5 French Church Street, Cork
24 Lower Abbey Street, Dublin 1

Text © Michael Scott, 1989
Illustrations © Joseph Gervin, 1989

First published by Sphere Books Limited in 1985 under the title
Tales from the Land of Erin, Volume 2, A Golden Dream. This edition
first published in 1989.

A CIP record for this book is available from the British Library.

ISBN 0 85342 867 0

10 9 8 7 6 5 4 3 2

FOR NICOLA DEVANEY: A SECOND EDITION

Printed in Ireland by Colour Books Ltd.

Contents

The Last Partholonian

The Partholonians came to the Land of Erin when the world was young, and Ireland was still a small, rocky island. They followed a leader called Partholon, who had been a prince in the land of Scythia before he had been forced to flee with his followers.

The Partholonians used their powerful magic to make the land grow. They pushed back the sea, exposing more and more ground and soon there was room enough for all, and the land was a rich and very beautiful place. But the fresh green land of Erin also attracted the terrible Fomorians, demons from the icy Northlands. And the Partholonians and the Fomorians fought together many times, until at last the Fomorians were defeated...

Tuan wandered across the battlefield on the morning after the last battle. The sun was still low in the sky, and cast long shadows across the trampled burnt earth. There were swords and shields, knives and spears, pieces of armour and torn rags of flags everywhere—but there were no bodies. The demons turned to dust once they were killed and the Partholonians had taken all their own dead men away.

Tuan shivered; it felt strange to be walking where only yesterday Partholon and his army had fought the terrible Cichal One-Foot, the leader of the Fomorians. He shaded his eyes with his hand and looked up at the low hill where the monster had finally been killed—but the only sign that anything had happened there was the long scorch mark on the grass where Cichal's tent had burnt down. Tuan shook his head slowly, thinking how terrible it had been and, pulling his cloak up around his ears, walked slowly across the grass towards the hill.

Tuan was the chief bard and storyteller of the Partholonians. His task was to make a story out of all the events that had happened to Partholon and his people since they had left their homeland. When night fell, he would stand up in the great hall and, in his rich strong voice, tell his stories, so that the people would remember. He would also sing about the great heroes and heroines, about the gods and goddesses and about the strange creatures and monsters that still wandered the world in those days.

Tuan was quite an old man now, and he had been Partholon's bard for many years, and before that he had been bard to Sera, Partholon's father. He was a very tall man, with snow-white hair, and a short, curled beard. His eyes were the colour of granite. He was supposed to know the entire history of the world and had once sung nine hundred different songs in one night for a bet.

But the song he was writing now would be his finest tale, he promised himself. It would be called *The Song of the Partholonians* and it would cover their flight from Scythia; their journey along the Middle Sea and out through the Pillars of Hercules, and then their travels up along the rocky coast of the land of the Iberians and across the stormy Bay of Biscay and finally to the tiny island which they would later call Banba. His story—his song—would finish with the battle with the demons, and the Partholonian victory. And that was why he was now walking through the battlefield. He wanted to see for himself just where the Last Battle had been fought, and what it might have felt like.

'Now, the demons gathered here,' Tuan said to himself, looking around. 'They had more men—well, demons really—down there, and they were all facing our men who were over there.' He pointed with his long-fingered hand across the field to another series of low hills.

'Now,' the old man continued, 'the demons were protected by their magical fog...' Tuan closed his eyes and he could almost see the thick red-grey fog rolling about down in the field below him. 'And the magical wind that our magicians made would probably have come in from the sea.' Tuan turned to look towards the east to where the distant blue glint of the sea could be seen. He imagined the wind gusting in from the sea, rich with the smell of the ocean, and whipping away the demons' protecting fog... and then the battle had begun.

Yes, Tuan nodded to himself, it was going to make a great story. He would sing it when the Victory Feast was held. But the feast would not be held until their leader Partholon recovered from the minor wound he had received in the battle. So, there was no real hurry, he had about a week or so.

Tuan crossed the field and walked up the low hill to where the Partholonians had gathered. Already, parts of his great song were beginning to come to him. He decided it would open with Partholon speaking to his men...

'Help me.'

Tuan stopped suddenly. He felt all the hairs on his head and in his beard begin to tingle and his heart began to pound harder and harder. Because that had not been a man's voice.

'Help me, please.'

The voice was harsh and rough, more of a bark than anything else. It sounded almost as if a dog had learned to speak.

'Help me.'

Tuan's first thought had been to run; after all, he was a bard, not a warrior. However, now that he had heard the voice speak again he thought that it sounded very weak. So, he carefully climbed up a low hill and looked down over the side.

And found that he was looking at a Fomorian, a demon. He didn't seem to be a very big demon, but he was very,

very ugly and more than a little bit frightening. He looked rather like a horse, but a man-shaped horse, with snake-like skin, that was all shimmering green scales. His head was very horse-like, except that his ears were too long and it had a black, snake-like tongue. Strangely, the demon also had the brightest blue eyes Tuan had ever seen.

The Fomorian was lying at the bottom of the hill in a hole with one of his long back legs twisted beneath himself. Because the ground was very soft and crumbled away every time he grabbed a handful to pull himself up, the demon was trapped.

The Fomorian looked up at Tuan with his bright blue eyes. 'Help me, please,' he said, in his rough, barking voice.

'But you're a demon!' Tuan said in surprise. 'Why should I help you?'

The demon shook his great head slowly. 'I don't know of any reason why you should help me,' he said, 'except that you might want to help another creature that is in pain.'

'And if I help you up, you'll probably kill me,' the bard said.

'I won't eat you,' the demon said. 'Besides, you're too old; the meat would be too tough and stringy.' Tuan looked insulted that no demon would even think about eating him. 'But will you help me up, please?' The demon paused and then he said, 'If you do, I will give you a great gift.'

'What is it?' Tuan asked greedily.

The Fomorian's eyes gleamed craftily. 'Help me out first and then I'll give it to you—it is something which few people in this world will ever have.'

'And you promise you won't eat me?'

'I promise.'

'Do you swear?' Tuan asked.

'I swear by my dead lord, Cichal One-Foot,' the Fomorian said.

'All right then. You stay there—well, you can't really go anywhere can you—and I'll go and get something to pull you out with.' Tuan hurried off to look for a length of rope or a long branch. However, he was half-way across the field when he spotted a long spear sticking into the grass. It was one of the Fomorian weapons, and was almost twice his height and made from a strange black wood. Tuan wrapped both hands around the thick shaft and pulled... and pulled... and pulled—and the spear came up out of the ground with a squelch. Tuan then dragged it back up the low hill. He leaned over and looked down.

'I've got something,' he said, and then he slid the spear down over the edge and into the hole.

The demon grabbed the spear and stuck it deep into the ground and then he began to pull himself up along the long length of wood. Tuan realised then just how big the Fomorian was—and he was huge. He looked like a horse standing up on its two hind legs. His two three-fingered front claws dug deep into the edge of the hole and in one smooth movement, he had pulled himself out of the hole. He lay stretched out on the grass, panting loudly. Tuan backed away slowly and carefully, although he knew that if the demon decided to eat him, he had little chance of escaping. The demon's bright blue eyes opened suddenly and he stared at the man.

'Thank you,' he said as quietly as he could, although it still sounded like a shout.

Tuan nodded without saying a word.

'You have saved my life—and now I will save yours,' the demon continued.

'But you promised you would not eat me,' Tuan said angrily.

'I'm not going to eat you,' the demon snapped. 'Now, listen to me. As we speak a terrible plague is beginning to kill all your people. It will start like an ordinary cold—a sore throat, runny nose, cough—but this is much more dangerous. The plague will kill all the Partholonians.'

'*Oh!*' Tuan could only whisper, shocked.

'All except you.'

'Me?' Tuan whispered.

'You will live; you will be the last Partholonian,' the demon said. 'I am going to save your life, and, at the same time, give you one of the most valuable gifts I can—that of almost eternal life. You, Tuan, are going to live for a long, long time.'

'But...?' Tuan began.

'There is very little time,' the demon said. 'Stand straight, close your eyes, put your hands down by your sides, and breathe easily.'

Tuan did as he was told and then for a long time nothing seemed to happen. He could hear his heart beating strongly in his chest, and he could feel the breeze on his face ruffling his hair and beard. And then a sudden thought struck him.

There was no breeze that morning!

Tuan tried to open his eyes, but found that he couldn't. And then he felt his skin tingling, as if pins and needles were dancing up and down his arms and legs. His skin

grew cold and then itchy, and then suddenly it felt hot and dry. His hair seemed to be standing on end and he could actually feel it growing, pushing its way out from his head and chin. He fell forward onto the ground, and now his arms began to ache and his legs felt rubbery, as if he had run a long distance. He heard his bones cracking and making strange popping sounds—and then, quite suddenly, it was all over, and he found that he could see again.

But now everything seemed different. All the colours seemed to be sharper and brighter—and everything seemed to be somehow smaller. Even the huge demon now looked no bigger than himself. 'What have you done to me?' he asked, or tried to say, because all that came out was a rough bellowing sound.

The Fomorian smiled, his huge mouth opening wide, showing his sharp yellow teeth. 'I have saved your life,' he

said. 'All the men and women on this island will shortly die—but you will not, because you are no longer a man.'

'What am I?' Tuan shouted, but all he heard was a roar. However, the demon seemed to understand his language.

'I have given you the shape of a wild ox,' he said. 'The spell will last for three hundred years, after that you will turn into a white horse for two hundred years; then you will turn into a golden eagle for another three hundred, and you will spend a final hundred in the shape of a salmon.' The demon was about to turn away, but then stopped. 'That is the best that I can do,' he said. 'If I were stronger or a better magician I might be able to give you a few hundred more years, but I'm afraid that nine hundred is the best I can do.'

'And what happens in nine hundred years' time?' Tuan shouted.

'Then you should turn back into a man,' the demon said, and, turning around, he ran quickly across the field and disappeared over a hill.

Tuan turned away and galloped in the opposite direction. Perhaps one of the magicians of the Partholonians might be able to turn him back into his human shape. He stopped only once, and that was when he reached a very small river. He bent his huge head down over the water and stared into it, wondering what he looked like. But, just as the demon had said, he was now a wild ox, a bull, with thick, pointed horns, and a smooth creamy-white skin. Only his large grey eyes still looked human.

Tuan galloped on then, but when he reached the Partholonian campsite, there was no one there. Everywhere was deserted, although the pots still bubbled on the fire, and it looked as if they had left only a few moments ago. He was wondering where they had gone when he caught a strange smell on the air. He didn't know what it was, but it was coming from the direction of the beach. He hurried down along the track that led down to the sea, his wide, wet nose wrinkling at the strange smell.

He was still wondering what it was when he reached the beach—and he found it, and the Partholonians. They were all lying about on the rough stony beach—dead. The plague the demon had been talking about had struck suddenly. There were some small boats floating in the waves just off shore, also with dead people in them, and Tuan realised that they must have been trying to escape when it had struck them down also.

And Tuan also realised that he was now the last Partholonian. The huge wild ox raised his head to the sky and bellowed sorrowfully.

Tuan lived for nine hundred years and more. He saw the light Nemedians, the dark evil Fir Bolgs, the magical Tuatha De Danann, and the human Milesians come to the tiny island. He saw the land grow green and strong beneath them, he watched the people come and go, and all the time he was learning. And when Tuan became a man again many hundreds of years later, he was the wisest man in all the land of Erin.

The Legend of Rock-a-Bill Island

Rock-a-Bill is an island off the lovely seaside town of Skerries on the east coast of Ireland. It has a curious shape, that of a large rock with a smaller rock just behind it. There is an ancient story told that it was formed because of a greedy and curious woman...

Boann sat back on the low wooden chair and watched her husband strapping on his sword and throwing his heavy woollen cloak over his shoulder.

'Where are you going?' she asked, although she had already guessed.

Nectain picked up a beautifully carved brooch and pinned his cloak across his left shoulder. He was a tall, well-built man, with dark brown hair and matching eyes. He ran his fingers through his hair and sighed. 'I've got to go and check on the Sidhe Well,' he said. He stretched and yawned. It was very early in the morning and the sun would not yet rise for another hour or so, but he had to be at the magic well by that time.

'Can I go?' Boann asked.

Nectain looked over at his wife. In the darkness he could barely make out her shape, although he knew if he could see, her face would be set in an angry frown. Every time he went to check on the well, she would ask the same question, and every time he would give the same answer.

'You know I cannot allow you to come,' he said. 'And you know why—it's too dangerous.'

'Why is it too dangerous?' Boann asked, and Nectain could imagine her bright blue eyes opening wide.

'Because it's a magical well,' Nectain said. 'Now, I've told you this a hundred times before.'

'I still don't see why I cannot go,' Boann said angrily.

'Look,' Nectain said softly, 'my family have guarded this well for many, many years. My great-great-grandfather was given the task by one of the last Tuatha De Danann to leave Erin. The fairy lord made him promise that only members of our family would come near the well, and he told him that if anyone else came near the magical waters something terrible would happen.'

'Well, I think that's silly,' Boann said.

'Well,' Nectain shrugged, 'it might be. But what happens if the magical waters lose their powers once someone else comes near? What will happen to all those people who need its water to cure them of their diseases and injuries?' He turned and looked out of the window, to where the sky was already beginning to lighten towards grey. 'I must go.' He bent and kissed his wife on the cheek and then, taking his long hunting spear from beside the door, hurried out into the cold, damp morning.

Boann stood by the door watching him disappear into the swirling morning mist. She knew he would meet his three brothers in the forest and then together the four men would make their way to the magical well and do whatever they usually did there.

Something brushed her leg and she looked down. It was Dabilla, her small pet dog. She stooped down and picked her up and held her close to her face. Boann ran her fingers through her pet's short wiry coat, wrinkling her nose at the smell of wet straw. 'I wonder what they do at the well?' she said softly to herself.

Dabilla wriggled about in her arms, trying to bite her round ear-rings. Boann gently pushed her head away.

'Unless of course there's some magic there that they don't want me to find out about. Perhaps there's some magic which would make me more powerful than they are...'

Dabilla whimpered and nuzzled her cold nose against her cheek. Boann squeaked with fright and almost absently rubbed her cheek against her shoulder. 'Next time, I think we'll follow them,' she decided. She held Dabilla up in the air with both hands. 'What do you think about that, eh?'

The dog barked happily.

Boann did not have long to wait before Nectain told her he had to visit the magical well again. Winter was coming on and a lot of people were falling ill with coughs and colds, and the water from the well was needed to cure these. Usually only a single drop of the water was needed, and when Nectain and his brothers returned they each bought with them two large water-skins full of the precious liquid. Riders would then carry it to all parts of the country, curing anyone suffering from any sort of illness.

So, two nights later, just before they pulled their thick woollen blankets and furs over their heads, Nectain told his wife that he had to be up early in the morning to go to the well. He paused then, waiting for her to argue with him, but was surprised when she said nothing.

'Are you not going to ask if you can come?' he said.

He heard Boann's hair rustle as she shook her head. 'No; you will only say no.'

'But you know why I have to,' Nectain said.

'I know,' she said.

Nectain settled down and pulled one of the furs up to his chin. 'Well, I'm glad we've got that settled.'

But he didn't see Boann smile in the darkness.

Nectain dressed quickly and quietly the following morning. Boann seemed to be still asleep and he didn't want to waken her. But as soon as he had gently closed the door behind him, her large eyes flickered open. She threw back the covers and padded barefoot to the window and looked out.

Outside it was still dark, but Boann could just about see Nectain hurrying down the path, making towards the woods. She saw three other shapes moving in the early morning darkness and knew that her husband had been joined by his brothers. They were going to the well.

It took Boann a few minutes to dress and tie her heavy travelling cloak around her shoulders. She strapped a small knife to her belt, just in case she should meet anything in the woods—although most of the animals that hunted by night would be settling down to rest for the day.

Boann pulled the wooden door open a fraction and peered out, but there was no sign of her husband or his brothers. So she slipped out into the dark, damp morning, and set off as quickly as she could in the same direction Nectain had taken.

Something yapped in the small wooden shed built onto the side of the round house, and then pushed its way out through a hole near the ground. It was Dabilla and she ran up to Boann, her tail wagging furiously, her short, sharp barks echoing in the morning quiet.

Boann knelt down and picked up the small dog. 'Shush, shush now,' she said urgently, 'they'll hear you.' She rubbed behind her pet's ears, making them twitch. 'You can come with me,' she said, 'but only if you promise to be quiet, and stay by my side at all times. Is that understood?' She looked into Dabilla's round, brown eyes.

Dabilla yapped.

'All right then.' Boann put the dog on the ground and then straightened up. 'We'd better hurry up if we're going to catch them.'

Boann, followed by Dabilla, hurried down the thin winding pathway that led into the forest. The forest was not a big one, but it was very old, and the Druids said that the trees here were amongst the oldest in the land of Erin. There was a fairy mound in the centre of the forest beneath which the last of the Tuatha De Danann were supposed to be living. But no one had ever seen the mound. There was probably a magical spell around it, hiding it from sight.

Once she entered the forest, Boann pulled up the hood of her cloak. The trees were heavy with mist that dripped and dropped down onto her head, with little sharp stings. Thick banks of white mist rolled slowly through the trees like smoke. It was a little frightening in a way, Boann thought, because it made it look as if the trees were moving. Even Dabilla seemed frightened and trotted so close to her ankles that she kept hitting the dog with her legs as she walked.

And then she heard a sound ahead of her. She stopped and Dabilla ran right into her legs and tumbled into a heap. Boann bent down and picked up the small dog. 'Sssh,' she whispered.

She heard the sound again; it was a sort of low droning noise, with short, sharp little breaks in it. For a few moments she didn't recognise what it was, but as she listened she suddenly realised that it was the sound of voices chanting.

Holding Dabilla tightly in her arms Boann crept towards the sound. It grew louder as she neared it, and soon she began to make out words, and then she recognised her husband's voice:

'... spirit of the waters, come out now and help us...'

Boann wondered who he was talking to; she thought that his voice sounded funny, sort of strange and strained. Carefully, she parted a clump of bushes and looked out towards the voices.

Boann found that she was staring across a small clearing, that was surrounded on three sides by the trees and on the fourth side by the tall heaped earth of the fairy mound. Through the trees to her lefthand side she could just about make out the grey-blue of the sea. And ahead of her was the fairy well.

It was a circle made up of quartz stones. The milky-white stones had been polished and smoothed and there was a strange stick-like writing carved into the stones in gold. There was also a flat cover of what looked like solid gold for the well, but this was lying on the grass away to one side.

Nectain and his three brothers were standing around the well. They had taken off their cloaks and had left them with their weapons near the base of one of the ancient trees. Boann was beginning to wonder why they were not even wearing their knives when she remembered that the Tuatha De Danann and the fairy folk could not bear to have iron near them. The four men had their arms raised high in the air, and were chanting quietly in the old language of the fairyfolk. When they stopped, Nectain would bow his head and speak to the well.

'Spirit of the Well, we need your healing waters once again. In return we promise to protect and guard you, as we have done these many years...'

For a long time nothing happened and then suddenly there was a sharp hissing sound from within the well and then drops of sparkling white water began to spit and snap upwards, only to fall back down into the well again. The white quartz began to change colour to a light brown, and then a pale red and finally a deep rich red colour.

When the four men saw the change come over the stones of the well, they stepped away and began to pick up the water-skins they had left close by. Then they waited.

For what seemed like a very long time nothing else happened and then slowly, so slowly that Boann was not sure when it had started, the colours within the stones began to dim and then just as slowly, they began to brighten. And then the waters in the well rose upwards in a thick solid pole that broke just above the tops of the trees and then fountained down in a glittering sparkle of colours. But all the water fell back into the well, and not a drop hit the ground.

Nectain and his brothers came forward slowly, their arms with the open water-skins held up. They edged the smooth bags under the falling water and very, very carefully filled them. When the skins had puffed up into solid balls, the men pulled the openings closed and then stepped back. When their eight bags were full, the fountain of water began to slip back into the well and the shifting colours in the stones began to settle down. Soon it had gone.

Nectain stepped up to the snow-white stones and raised his hands high. 'Thank you Spirit of the Well for this healing, magical water. We thank you on behalf of all the people of Erin. My brothers and I will guard you always.' With the help of one of his brothers Nectain pulled the heavy golden cover back up onto the stones and dropped it into place. And then, without a word, they picked up their full water-skins, gathered up their cloaks and weapons and headed back along the trail that led towards Nectain's fort.

Boann waited until there was neither sight nor sound of the four men and then she stepped out from behind the bushes and walked over to the well. She ran her fingers down the smooth stones, and they felt cool and silky to her touch.

'I wonder if I could lift the cover,' she said to herself. It looked heavy and solid, and it had taken two men to lift it up, but perhaps she might be able to shift it to one side so that she could look down into the magical waters.

Boann put Dabilla on the ground and then, placing both hands against the edge of the golden cover, she pushed.

Nothing happened.

Boann tried again. She dug her heels into the damp grass and heaved with all her might...and slowly, slowly, the heavy cover shifted with a grumbling, grating sound. It moved further and then one edge slipped out of the lip it was resting against and the cover suddenly shifted and tilted and then stuck. Boann tried to shift it, but it was stuck fast.

Now her husband and his brothers would know someone had been at the well. She picked up Dabilla and turned to hurry back home. If she reached there before Nectain, no one would know she had been at the well. But before she hurried back down the winding track, she stopped. She wondered just what lay within the well. So Boann looked into the dark opening.

For a few moments she could see nothing—it just looked like an ordinary well. And then she spotted something small and red far, far down in the water. She looked again, and then saw that there were two of them. And then her heart gave a thump, because she suddenly knew what the two small red things were.

They were eyes.

Boann turned to run then, but she was too late. The water rose up in a solid pillar with a roar like an angry beast. There was a shape in the water—the shape of a tall, thin, wild-haired woman, with cat-like eyes. She pointed at Boann and water shot out from the well and splashed her leg, her arm and in her eye—and the water was hot!

Boann screamed in fright and pain. She turned and ran towards the sea, hoping the icy sea-water would cool her burns. Dabilla ran along behind her, yapping and snarling, and when Boann looked over her shoulder to see what her pet was barking at, she found that the Spirit of the Well was chasing her. Boann screamed again and tried to run even faster.

The Spirit of the Well crashed through the forest in a foaming sheet of water, uprooting trees and bushes, picking up stones and boulders and carrying them along. The Spirit roared and the sound was like the crash of a wave on a rocky beach.

Boann crunched into the sand and had just about reached the sea when the Spirit of the Well caught up with her. It swept up Dabilla first and then crashed forward and grabbed the woman. Boann screamed and Dabilla yapped but the sound was lost in the roaring of the water. The Spirit of the Well tossed them high into the air and then flung them out across the waves, so that they skipped and bounded like flat stones.

And then the Spirit said something in her own watery language, and a change began to come over the woman and the dog. As they bounced, their shapes began to change, to harden and become rough and jagged. They began to grow. Before they finally sank into the waves they had both changed into craggy islands.

There was nothing Nectain or anyone else could do to change his wife back into her own form. None of the magicians or druids were as powerful as the Spirit of the Well and she was using the most powerful, oldest magic of all—the fairy magic.

So the larger of the two islands was called after Boann's pet, Dabilla, and in the Irish language it was called Cnoc Dabilla. But time passed and over the years it became known as Rock-a-Bill.

The King Of the Cats

Cats are strange, mysterious creatures, having a magic and a beauty all their own. In some countries they have even been worshipped as gods. In Ireland there is supposed to be one particular cat who is the king of all the cats in Erin. He is a wise and ancient creature who knows and guards all the hoards of fairy gold in the country.

This is a story about Ri, the king of the cats, and the time he almost lost the last of his nine lives...

Ri pressed his belly to the soft grass and without a sound, crept up the river bank. Carefully, very carefully, he stretched out one paw and allowed his long talons to slide into place, and then he parted the last few blades of grass. The orange cat looked down into the river. The fish was still there.

Ri had spotted the silver trout a few moments earlier. The fish had been leaping and splashing in the stream and, with the sun sparkling on her silvery scales, turning them all the colours of the rainbow, she looked very lovely— and very tasty too. Lunch, Ri thought.

The trout leapt again, wriggled about in the air for a single second and then fell back into the river with a splash. Droplets of water splattered Ri's coat, and his whiskers wrinkled in annoyance. He wasn't really too fond of water.

The fish jumped again, nearer this time, and Ri tensed. Just a few inches closer and he would be able to make a quick grab...

The fish jumped right in front of the cat and Ri slashed out with his talons. He missed by a fraction. But the trout, twisting wildly in mid-air, smacked the cat across the head with its tail. Ri jumped up, snarling in astonishment and anger; how dare she do that to him! He was the king of the cats! He stood on the river bank and spat at the fish, but it was already falling back into the water. It fell with a huge splash that sent water stinging into the cat's eyes. He screamed—and then snarled as he toppled off the bank and into the river where he was immediately swept away.

The trout swam away, smiling quietly to herself, in the way that fish do.

Gerard leaned over the bridge and dropped a handful of stones one by one into the water beneath. The river here was calm and slow-moving and he watched the stone splash into the water and then drift slowly to the sandy bottom. Ripples would form then and spin outwards in slowly widening circles and he would try to drop the next stone in the centre of the circle. It was a game he played every day on his way home from school.

The young boy picked up his last stone and stretched out his arm, over the circle that was rippling across the water. He closed one eye—and dropped the stone. There was a splash—a bull's-eye—and then something large and orange floated down the river, right through his ripples.

It was a cat!

Gerard watched it drift slowly down the river for a few moments. It was struggling to keep its head above water, but even as he watched, he saw that it was getting weaker. If he didn't get to it soon it would drown.

Gerard ran back over the bridge and then slipped down along a thin track that ran along the edge of the river. It wasn't a very safe path; it was overgrown with nettles and bushes, and parts of it had crumbled away into the water. The young boy ran along as quickly as he could, his neat bundle of school books, which were tied up with string and slung over his shoulder, banging and thumping against his back as he ran. He jumped over tree roots and pushed his way through thick bushes. Soon he was scratched and cut, but he didn't feel the pain in his rush. He knew he had to reach the bend in the river before the cat, because once around the bend, the river widened and he would have no chance of rescuing the poor creature. He saw the water sparkling through the trees on his right-hand side now—and he knew that this was where the river curved.

There were two large flat stones in the water where the river curved. Some of the other boys used them as a short cut, but they were usually wet and slippery and Gerard had never used them. But now the young boy stepped carefully onto the first stone and then crouched down on his hands and knees. He could see the orange bundle of fur in the river ahead of him. It was spinning around slowly, sometimes even dipping below the water, but it was coming closer.

Gerard tensed.

The river seemed to carry the cat along with a sudden burst of speed, because suddenly it was beside him. He made a grab for it, and missed. Another wild grab and he caught its tail. The shock nearly pulled him off the stone, but he held on with one hand while holding tightly to the cat's tail with the other. It gave a watery squeak.

Still holding the creature by the tail, Gerard stood up and then jumped back onto dry land. He then sat down on the ground with a sigh. He suddenly realised that he was soaked through, and that his cuts and scratches were stinging. He also found that his legs were trembling. He looked at the cat. It was a very ordinary looking cat; with dull orange-coloured fur which was now plastered tight to its body, making it look like a drowned rat, rather than a cat. Gerard smiled at the thought.

'What's so funny?'

The boy jumped up and looked around, but there was no one behind him. 'Who's there?' he said, his voice shaking a little.

'I'm here,' the voice said again. It was a rough rasping sort of voice.

'Where?' Gerard whispered again.

'*Here!*' the voice insisted, with a snarl.

Gerard looked down at the cat. It was sitting back on its haunches, carefully licking its paws. Its sharp green eyes were looking straight at him. The boy pointed at the cat and opened his mouth to say something, but nothing would come out except a yelp of astonishment.

'Yes, me!' the cat said.

'But... but you're a cat!' Gerard said.

'Yes,' the cat said, with what might have been a cat grin. 'Have you never heard a cat speak before?'

The boy could only shake his head.

The cat cocked its small head to one side. 'Well, I'm not your ordinary sort of cat,' he said. 'My name is Ri, and I am the King of the Cats.'

'The King of the Cats?' Gerard whispered.

'Yes, you must have heard of me,' Ri said.

The boy nodded. He had often heard stories about the King of the Cats—but he had never believed them.

Ri continued cleaning his fur. 'Thank you for saving my life; I would certainly have drowned.'

'I thought cats had nine lives,' Gerard said.

Ri smiled, showing his small, sharp white teeth. 'I am very old now,' he said. 'I've used up my other eight lives, this is my ninth.'

'How long will you live for?'

Ri shrugged. He lifted one of his front legs and allowed his talons to slide in and out. 'As long as I don't die by accident,' he said, 'I could live for another hundred years or more. You see,' he continued, 'I have certain magical powers. I was the first cat to come to the land of Erin from the land of the Nile when this world was very young.'

'You came from Egypt?' Gerard said in a whisper.

Ri nodded. 'I was born on the island of Meroe on the Nile in the land of Egypt. When a great flood threatened my country, my mistress, the Princess Caesir Banba, with a few of her closest friends and followers, sailed to the edge of the world in search of a safe place. They landed on this land. It was only a tiny island then, of course, but the princess had her sorceress make the land bigger, and many years later when the Partholonians came, they too made the land grow.'

'What happened to the Princess?' Gerard asked.

'A terrible disease killed them all,' Ri said sadly. 'Only I alone remained, but when later invaders came to this land, I made sure that they called this land after my mistress...'

'Banba!' Gerard said excitedly. 'That was one of the oldest names for Ireland.'

Ri nodded, 'It was.' He rose slowly and carefully to his feet and then stretched, arching his back almost into a half circle. 'I must go now,' he said.

'Will I see you again?' Gerard asked.

The King of the Cats shook his head. 'No, I don't think so. But you will hear from me,' he added.

'What do you mean?' Gerard asked, but Ri just shook his head.

'Are you fond of fish?' he asked.

Gerard nodded, puzzled. 'Why?' he asked.

But the cat just shook his head again and would say nothing more.

When Gerard reached home, both cut and scratched, his clothes torn and dirty, his mother was so angry that she sent him to bed immediately. And neither she nor his father would believe his story.

However, the following day on his way home from school, Gerard stopped as usual to drop some stones into the water. But when the first stone splashed into the river, a large silver trout hopped up, wriggling and squirming. Without thinking, Gerard leaned out over the bridge and caught the fish. It flapped about in his hands for a few moments and then lay still.

Gerard brought it home for his mother to cook for his father's supper, but when she opened the fish, she found a huge green emerald inside in a little leather bag that had a cat's paw print stamped on it!

King of the Birds

The wren is the smallest of the birds, and yet it is sometimes called the King of the Birds. How the wren became the king shows that size and strength are not always everything...

The trees were lined with birds. Every branch was bowed down beneath the weight of the gathered flocks. There were sparrows and cuckoos, robins and blackbirds, thrushes and starlings, pigeons and magpies, swallows and tits. In the lower branches there were some of the bigger birds, the falcons and ospreys, seagulls, cormorants and one other, a golden winged eagle.

They had all assembled to choose their King.

Relige, the barn owl, opened his huge eyes and blinked at the gathered birds. He would referee the race, and make sure that everyone observed the rules. He flapped his wings a few times, and gradually the muttering and chattering and twittering died down, and hundreds of pairs of eyes, small and hard and black, or big and bright, turned to look at him.

'Now, youuu all know the ruuules,' he hooted. 'Whoooever flies the highest will be king of all the birds in Ireland. Anyone found cheating will be immediately disqualified,' he added sternly, looking over at the magpies and rooks. Beside him the two swans who would also act as judges tried to look stern.

'Now, are youuu all ready?'

Wings opened and closed, and for a moment it looked as if the green trees had come alive with splashes of colour as the different feathers shone in the early morning light.

'Any last questions?' Relige asked.

There was a sudden movement on the lower branches of an ancient oak tree and bronze feathers ruffled and a sharp-beaked head thrust forward. Bright golden eyes turned to look at the assembled birds and then turned back to Relige.

Iolar the golden eagle ruffled his magnificent feathers and spread his wings to their fullest extent. 'Will I be crowned king when I win?' he asked rudely.

'How do you know you'll win?' Snag, the magpie asked, his hard black eyes darting back and forth. Snag never looked anyone in the face for long.

Iolar laughed in a powerful cawing. 'I am a golden eagle,' he said, 'I am the largest, the most powerful, the most beautiful bird here. I deserve to win.' He closed his wings with a snap, the wind knocking a few of the smaller birds from the branches above his head.

Relige raised one smoothly feathered wing. 'But youuu must remember, Iolar, a king must be kind and considerate. Speed and power and beauty are not everything.'

'But I will still win,' Iolar insisted.

'Now, youuu must all remember,' Relige the barn owl said, 'this is not a race. It is a competition to see whooo can fly the highest. Sooo, take youuur time.' He paused and raised his wings again.

'Nearly ready...

'Ready...

'Fly!'

The flock of birds took off in a huge feathered cloud, rising up into the morning sky with the sound of a thousand

pairs of hands clapping loudly. The leaves of the trees twisted and turned and blew off in the breeze and branches shook and rattled as if in a storm.

Relige and Eala and Aela the swans stared up at the flock of birds, and they each wondered who would win.

Iolar, probably, they thought.

Iolar's huge wings beat smoothly and strongly, pushing him upwards all the time. Already, he had left most of the smaller birds behind, and as he looked down he could see that some of them were beginning to return to the ground, convinced that it would be useless to go any further.

He was going to win. He was going to be the king of all the birds in Ireland.

He continued climbing up. Beneath him the ground curved away smoothly at the edges, the bright green of the land turning into the sharp blue of the sea. He could see the tiny patchwork squares of the fields, and the thin white threads of the roads. He flew through clouds, through white fluffy balls that always looked so warm and soft but which were always so cold and damp.

Soon, there was no one beneath him. A sea-gull had hung on for a surprisingly long time, but had given up some time in the early afternoon, and drifted lazily back down to the ground. He was alone in the sky. He was the king of the birds.

On the ground Relige and the two swans looked up to the distant black dot high, high, high in the sky. All around them the birds were resting, lining the branches and bushes, gathered in small groups on the ground. They too were all looking up. Iolar had won.

Iolar closed his wings with a snap. He was going no further, and he had won anyway. But as he began to fall back towards the earth, he felt something moving in the feathers on his back, and then a tiny voice said, 'Thank you,' and he twisted his head in time to see a tiny wren take flight off his back.

Iolar shouted and opened his wings, beating them furiously to catch the wind. But already he had fallen down quite far, and the wren who had hitched the ride on his back was far, far above him. 'Come back,' he shouted, 'come back. That's not fair. I've won.'

But the wren only continued flying higher and higher, and now the eagle's wings were tired and he began to slip nearer and nearer to the ground. 'Just you wait,' he warned.

Iolar sped towards the ground, only opening his wings a few feet above the soil. They snapped him to a stop and he slid to a halt, his long talons digging into the earth. 'Tell him that's not fair,' he shouted at the barn owl and the two swans. 'Tell him that's not allowed.'

Relige smiled and looked from the furious eagle up to the tiny spot that was the wren far above their heads. He looked back to the two swans and they whispered together for a few moments

'Well?' Iolar demanded.

'Being a king means not only being big and strong and powerful, it also means being clever and thinking ahead and planning. Dreolin the wren did that. We will crown *him* king of the birds.'

And that is how the tiny wren outwitted the huge eagle and became King of the Birds.

March, April and the Brindled Cow

In the calendar, April only has thirty days, but March has thirty-one. However, it was not always so, because in the old days, April had one day more than March. Here is the story how March got the extra day from April...

Bo was a cow; a beautiful shining-coated, sleek animal. Her coat was snow white with small, almost perfectly round brown circles on it; she was what the country people called a Brindled Cow. She was so lovely that the farmer gave her special treatment, and she had a small outhouse all to herself. Sometimes he would exhibit her at the country fairs, but she soon won so many prizes that he had to stop, because the other farmers complained that their prize cows never won anything.

And then one day March Many-weathers saw Bo, the Brindled Cow. It was the first day of the month and he was sweeping in from the north with a chill wind and a few icy showers tucked in his sack, ready to spread them across the land of Erin. He stopped and hovered above a low mountain while he watched the Brindled Cow. Her coat was so lovely that he decided he must have it; he would have a new weather-sack made out of it. He sent a quick shower scurrying down the mountain that quickly drenched the animal, and then he watched the water glisten on her smooth waterproof coat.

'I must have that coat,' March said to himself. But what he didn't know was that his voice echoed down the mountainside and the Brindled Cow heard him.

Bo looked up and saw the dark, grey-looking cloud sitting on the mountain top, and she suddenly knew what March was going to do. 'He will send an icy wind sweeping down here and strip my shining coat off me,' she said. So she turned and ran for the forest.

March saw the Brindled Cow begin to run towards the trees. He knew that if she reached them his icy, cutting breezes would not be as powerful and he might not be able to have her beautiful spotted coat. So, gathering up his storms, icy rains, hailstones and winds, he launched himself down the mountainside after the cow. Trees were flattened as he passed and bushes were uprooted. Even the farmers in the fields and the shepherds on the mountains with their flocks, ran for cover as the March wind passed, and they all wondered what he was chasing.

Bo looked over her shoulder and saw the grey storm clouds racing after her. March was fast, she knew, and you never knew just what he was going to do. One moment he could be bright, warm and with the sun shining and the next, it could be cold, wet and icy. But another few feet and she should be within the trees, and she hoped she would be safe there.

March saw Bo race into the first trees and increased his speed. He had to catch her before she got too far inside the forest. He stripped the moss from stones and the bark from trees as he sped past. Houses swayed from side to side and the roofs of thatched cottages were pulled off in one piece—but March was too late. Bo galloped into the forest just as the first chill winds were stretching out greedy fingers to rub her coat.

Once she got into the forest, she headed for the thickest bushes and the strongest trees, because she guessed that March would send little breezes in after her. When she reached the centre of the forest, she stopped and leaned against an ancient oak tree and caught her breath.

March hung around outside the forest, waiting to see if she would come out, but when nothing happened after a while, he sent a few small breezes in to see what was happening. They came out a few seconds later.

'Well?' March rumbled.

'She's in there,' one of the breezes said in a high-pitched breathless voice.

'But you will never fit,' another breeze said, 'she's in the very centre of the forest, surrounded by thick bushes on all sides and with strong trees protecting her also.'

March considered for a while, and then he asked, 'Could I go in from the top?'

'No,' a breeze squeaked in a gusty voice, 'the branches over her head are all twisted and grown together; you would never manage to squeeze through.'

March raged and swore, tramping around, blowing down the occasional building, and uprooting a field of crops in temper, but in the end he decided he would hang around for a while and see if Bo came out.

But the days passed and there was still no sign of the Brindled Cow.

When March's time was just about up, April came to see him. Now April Showers was not so rough as March, although she could be very tough, but she was usually a kindly month, and it was mostly her work which brought out the flowers in May.

'What are you doing here?' April asked March. 'You should be ready to go home by now.'

'I need an extra day,' March said quickly to April, 'will you lend me one of yours?'

'What do you want it for?' April asked.

'Look, I just need one extra day, I'll give it back to you, I promise.'

'Well if you promise not to be too rough with it,' April said, and she gave him one of her days.

But the poor Brindled Cow, thinking that March was over and gone, came galloping out of the forest into the fields again, laughing to herself.

'Hello April,' she said.

'It's not April,' March roared, 'it's still me!' And with a few cutting breezes, he stripped Bo of her beautiful brindled coat!

March never did give that extra day back to April, although she asked him for it on many occasions. And country people still call the last day of March and the first day of April 'Brindled Cow Days', meaning that the weather can still be very changeable.

The Fox and the Hedgehog

Everyone knows the story about the tortoise and the hare, but very few people know that Irish storytellers were telling a very similar story many hundreds of years ago...

Sionnach the fox looked up suddenly, his pointed ears twitching, his wet black nose wrinkling. Something was coming. He lay flat on the ground and his brown coat so matched the piles of golden fallen leaves that it was impossible to see him. His nose wrinkled again, testing the damp forest air, sorting out the different smells: the wet ground, the rotting leaves, and the sap of the different trees. He recognised the smell of birds and insects and, faint and in the distance, he caught the hated smell of smoke, the sign of man. But it was the final, different odour that he couldn't make out. It was a musty, musky, dry sort of smell, and yet it also smelt damp and earthy.

Something rustled through some dry leaves and Sionnach froze. He felt his heart beginning to beat and he had the sudden urge to sneeze—but that always happened at times like this. More leaves rustled and then what looked like a small walking ball of leaves stopped right in front of the fox's hiding place. For a moment Sionnach didn't know what it was, but then he suddenly recognised it—it was a hedgehog.

Dinner, Sionnach thought, and he leaped out right in front of the hedgehog.

Grainne squealed with fright, and then she rolled herself up into a tiny spiny ball. What a stupid fox, she thought.

Sionnach looked at the ball of spines in front of him and had second thoughts. Perhaps it had not been such a good idea just to jump out in front of the hedgehog like this. But he decided to do the best he could. 'Well, I have you now,' he said, grinning.

'Have you?' Grainne asked, her voice sounding muffled because her head was tucked down and into her body.

Sionnach padded around the ball and tapped it with his paw. *Ouch!* Those spines hurt! What was he going to do with the hedgehog?

'What are you going to do with me?' Grainne asked, almost as if she could read his mind.

'Well, I'm going to eat you of course,' Sionnach said.

'How?' she asked.

But Sionnach didn't answer, because he wasn't too sure himself.

After a while, Grainne said, 'Why don't you let me go— I'm sure there will be something tastier along in a little while.'

But Sionnach stubbornly shook his head. 'No, I'm not going to let you go. I'm going to eat you.'

'You will only hurt yourself,' Grainne said, with what sounded like a sigh.

The fox looked at the sharp spines and thought again. He had once run into a thorn bush when he was being chased by a pack of dogs, and he still remembered how sharp those thorns had been. Eating the hedgehog would be like chewing a thorn bush.

'Why can't you let me go?' Grainne asked.

Sionnach shook his head again. 'What would happen if the other foxes heard about it?' he asked. 'They would only laugh at me, and say I couldn't even eat a simple hedgehog. I have my reputation to think of,' he added proudly.

'A lot of foxes won't eat hedgehogs,' she said after a while, 'not unless they're very hungry. Are you very hungry?'

'Well not very. But I wouldn't mind some dinner now.'

'Well, I'm terribly sorry, but I am not on the menu for today. Now I can lie here all day, and all night too, but you'll have to leave. So, you're just wasting you're time.'

Sionnach sat back on his haunches and looked at the spiky ball in front of him. If he turned her over, he might be able to... but no, he shook his head. To do that would mean either using his paws, or his nose, and he didn't want to get either of those spiked. So, what he would have to do would be to trick the lady hedgehog. He closed his eyes and wondered just what he could do.

Time passed, and the sun moved slowly across the heavens, sending slanting beams in through the branches. The autumn leaves turned bright red and gold, orange and bronze in the light, and it gave everything a rich, warm glow. Two of the last butterflies of summer chased each other through the trees, the sun turning their red and black wings to brilliant spots of colour. They twisted around, darting and turning, resting for a few seconds on the warm branches of the trees before darting off again.

Sionnach watched them, their beautiful shapes and colours distracting him from the still curled-up hedgehog on the ground between his two front paws. And then he had an idea. He gave a short, sharp bark with excitement.

'I've had an idea,' he said.

There was no movement or sound from the hedgehog— well almost no sound. The fox's sharp ears caught a low buzzing sort of sound, and it seemed to be coming from the hedgehog. He turned his head and brought his sharp ears down close to the small bundle... and found that it was snoring!

'Wake up,' he barked.

'I'm awake, I'm awake,' Grainne grumbled. 'What's wrong with you now?'

'I've had an idea,' Sionnach said.

'So?'

'I'm going to let you go,' the fox said quickly.

'Well I don't believe you,' Grainne said, just as quickly. 'It's a trick or a trap.'

'Why would I do that?' Sionnach asked in his most innocent voice.

'Because you're hungry and you want to eat me,' the hedgehog said.

'Well...' the fox began.

'Well that?' Grainne demanded.

'Well, I'm going to let you go. I am going to count up to one hundred and then I'm going to come after you. If I catch you, then I'll eat you; but if you reach the river before I catch you then I'll let you go.'

'How do I know I can trust you?' Grainne asked.

Sionnach looked hurt. 'Because I'm a fox, and while we may be tricky and maybe we sometimes don't tell the full truth, we never tell lies.'

'So, if I can reach the river, then I'm safe?' Grainne asked.

Sionnach nodded. 'That's right.'

'And you'll count to a hundred first—all the way to a hundred?'

'All the way,' he promised.

'When do we start?' she asked.

'As soon as you wish,' he said.

Suddenly the hedgehog was up and running—well, waddling really — as quickly as she could into the forest. She was so quick that the fox was not quite ready, and she was already disappearing down along a winding track before he started counting.

'One... two... three... four. One... two... three... four.'

Foxes can only count to four—one for each paw. So Sionnach did a quick sum and divided four into one hundred and came up with twenty-five. He began to scratch little marks in the ground with his nails for every 'one, two, three, four'. When he had twenty-five scratches he would go after the hedgehog.

Meanwhile, Grainne had no sooner lost sight of the fox when she stopped and crept into the thickest thorn bush she could find and quickly wormed her way into its very centre. She knew that she could not outrun the quicker fox, and she knew that he would be able to follow her scent there, but what she was hoping was that he would not be able to get in, and would eventually get tired and go away. Once she was in the very heart of the bush, she gave a huge sigh of relief.

'Is something the matter?' a thin, high voice asked above her head.

Grainne looked up to find a sparrow peering down through the branches.

'A fox is after me,' Grainne said, and quickly told the sparrow what had happened.

'Oh, I know that fox,' the sparrow—whose name was Gealbhan—said, 'and once he finds out you're in here, he will sit outside for days and days. He doesn't give up easily.'

'But I've got to get home to my little ones,' Grainne said, 'I can't sit here for days. What am I going to do?'

Gealbhan cocked his small head to one side for a few minutes and then he said, 'Do you know of any other hedgehog living near the river?'

'Well there is my sister, Grainneog,' Grainne said. 'She lives in a tree stump right on the river bank. That's where I was going before the fox stopped me.'

'Well then,' Gealbhan said, 'here's what we'll do then...'

'One, two, three, four. One, two, three, four.' Sionnach took a deep breath and said, as quickly as he could, 'One, two, three, four. Here I come!'

The fox dashed down along the path, his long, low body weaving through the trees and bushes, his bushy tail flowing out behind him. At first he could catch faint traces of hedgehog scent, but after a while all traces of it disappeared. He began to get a little worried when there was neither sight nor smell of the creature, but he soon began to pick up the damp smell of the river, and he decided he would go there first before turning back to check and see if she had decided to hide along the track. He was quite sure he was going to catch her, because of course, there was no way such a small, slow creature could outrun him, Sionnach the fox.

The fox ran out of the bushes and skidded to a halt in the soft ground of the river bank. He stopped—right in front of a hedgehog. 'What took you so long?' she asked, and curled up into a tight ball.

Sionnach looked at her in amazement for long moments before silently trotting away, shaking his head. He never did work out just how the hedgehog had beaten him to the river bank, and he never tried to eat a hedgehog again.

Of course, all that had happened was that Gealbhan the sparrow had flown to Grainneog, Grainne's sister, and told her what had happened, and she met the fox when he arrived. Foxes might be very clever, but they can be very stupid sometimes also.

The Dog and the Leprechaun

Have you ever noticed how cats and dogs sometimes sit up and look at something that is not there? Have you ever seen a dog barking at nothing? And have you ever wondered why?

Perhaps it is because the animals can see the fairy folk coming and going all the time, while humans can only see the Little People at certain times. The fairy folk often do favours for cats and dogs, and help them whenever they can...

Tom-Tom lay in the tall grass and watched the bright green frog sitting on the river bank ahead of him. His long tail thumped gently on the hard ground, and his ears twitched at the flies that buzzed around. Tom-Tom was a dog; he was mostly collie, but there was also some spaniel in him, and his tail was certainly borrowed from a red setter. And, like all collies and spaniels he was very, very curious, and this often landed him in trouble. Right now he was interested in the frog.

The large green frog sat on the river bank, staring out across the gently flowing waters with his round, surprised eyes. He sat quite still, and his colour blended in almost perfectly with the long grass and reeds that grew along the water's edge. He was aware of the fish gliding silently beneath the surface of the water; he watched the tiny insects dart and buzz through the air; he felt the breeze on his skin, and he also knew that there was a dog hiding in the bushes watching him. He wasn't sure why the dog was watching him—it couldn't be to eat, because frogs really don't taste too good. He saw the leaves of the bush begin to tremble and knew that the stupid dog was preparing to jump. So, he gave a little 'rivvit', and hopped closer to the water's edge.

Tom-Tom saw the frog begin to move and knew he'd better make his own move soon. So, with a little half-bark, he leaped out of the bushes and ran down the river bank towards the frog.

The frog gave another 'rivvit' and hopped out onto a broad green leaf, and if you looked very quickly, you might have thought that he stuck his tongue out at the dog.

Tom-Tom however, was in trouble. He saw the frog jump out onto the leaf and suddenly realised how close he was to the water. He dug his claws in and tried to stop, but the bank was very muddy here, and he just kept sliding, leaving four little grooves of mud behind him. He gave a short bark of alarm and fright as his legs shot out from under him and he continued sliding down on his belly. Out of the corner of his eye, Tom-Tom saw the frog jump onto another wide leaf and hop away, and he had an idea. Just before he slid into the water in a pile of mud, Tom-Tom bunched his legs beneath him and jumped out onto one of the broad flat leaves.

He realised it wasn't really such a good idea when the leaf promptly folded up around him and he went straight down. That was the last time he chased a frog, he promised himself. Tom-Tom felt his feet touch the muddy bottom of the river and then he began to float upwards. His head broke through the surface and he blinked water from his wide brown eyes and looked around. He was surprised to find that he was already far out in the middle of the river, and then he realised that the current was pulling him away. Tom-Tom gathered his four legs together and began to paddle furiously for the shore, but it was no use, the current was too strong and kept pulling him back into the middle of the river. He was trapped, and unless he managed to get out soon, he would surely drown.

About a mile away Seamus Ban was sitting in the shade of a willow tree, fishing. Not that you would have noticed the little man there, because Seamus Ban was a leprechaun, one of the Little People. He was dressed in what he called his 'old clothes' today: a dark brown short coat over a green vest and dark green leggings that had a hole in one knee. He was wearing a dirty three-cornered hat, and only his shoes, which were shining black leather with huge silver buckles, looked new—which they probably were, because Seamus Ban was the finest shoe-maker in all Erin.

Seamus Ban had taken off one of his shoes to fish. He was lying on his back, with his hat resting on his face, and one leg sticking out over the river. And tied to his knobbly big toe was a piece of string which dangled into the river. If a fish took the bait, he would feel the pull on his toe and wake up. That was what was supposed to happen, although the last time he had done that, a huge salmon had come along and swallowed the bait—and kept going! The leprechaun had been dragged shouting and spluttering for miles, bouncing and skipping along the surface of the water like a flat stone, before he had managed to slip free. So today, he had taken the precaution of tying a length of rope around his waist and onto the branches of one of the bushes behind him.

No sound came from the leprechaun—noises were supposed to frighten the fish— but if you listened very carefully, you might have heard tiny, snorting snores coming from beneath the hat, and if you looked very carefully, you might have seen the hat rising and falling ever so slightly with each snore.

Tom-Tom meanwhile, was getting desperate. The river was becoming faster and faster all the time, and he was tiring quickly. He had to get out of the water soon. Suddenly a bend in the river brought him in close to the shore. He lifted his head as high as he could and snapped at passing branches, but all he got was a mouth full of leaves.

And then he spotted the white stick. Tom-Tom had no time for second thoughts, and his jaws closed with a click over the stick!

The other end of the stick gave a high-pitched scream and went shooting up into the air, dragging the dog with it. It gave Tom-Tom a terrible fright, and he almost let go, but his jaws seemed to be locked around the thin white stick. He landed on the river bank with a thump which knocked out what little wind was left in him. But when he opened his eyes, he got another terrible fright: the thin white stick was attached to a small, dark man. The stick was his leg! Tom-Tom's mouth opened with astonishment and then he watched the little man go dancing around and around, hopping on one foot, holding the other in both hands.

'My foot, my foot, my foot,' he kept saying with every jump.

'I'm very sorry...' Tom-Tom began.

But the little man didn't want to know. 'Let me tell you,' he said, still hopping, 'this is the first day off I've had in... well, in a few hundred years at least. And what happens? I'll tell you what happens. Some mad dog comes along and chews off my leg.'

'I have not chewed off your leg,' Tom-Tom said indignantly.

'Well, you nearly did,' the small man snapped, 'There's very little difference.'

'There would be if I chewed your leg off,' Tom-Tom smiled. 'You wouldn't be able to hop around like that if I did, for a start.'

The leprechaun thought about that for a moment and then he smiled also. 'Well, I suppose you're right. Now, would you like to tell me how you came to be chewing on my leg in the first place?' The small man sat down on the grass and examined his leg. Luckily the skin was not even broken, although Tom-Tom's teeth marks could be clearly seen just below the bony knee.

So Tom-Tom sat on the river bank and told the leprechaun how he had come to be floating down the river in the first place, while the leprechaun wandered around looking for a dock leaf to put on the bruise.

'I thought dock leaves were only used for nettle stings,' Tom-Tom said when he was finished.

'They are, but I've forgotten what you use for a bruise; half an apple or potato or something like that,' the leprechaun said. 'Oh,' he said then, 'you never told me your name.'

'Tom-Tom,' the dog said. 'I'm called that because I'm always thumping my tail on the ground and it makes a tom-tom sound.'

'I'm Seamus Ban, the leprechaun.'

'I am sorry I bit your leg,' the dog said.

'Och, but there's no harm done, and I'm glad I was able to help you.' He looked down at the piece of string still tied to his big toe. 'Well, I don't suppose I'll catch anything today. I'd better be getting along.' He began to pull on his shoe.

Tom-Tom nodded. 'Well, thank you again. You've saved my life. Perhaps I will be able to help you some day.'

Seamus Ban nodded. 'Aye, perhaps.'

And then the leprechaun and the dog trotted off in different directions.

Peter Casey stopped so suddenly that his cousin walked straight into him, banging his nose on the back of Peter's head.

'My nose, my nose,' he shouted, clapping both hands to his face and falling to the ground.

Peter immediately dropped to his knees by his side and pressed a grubby hand across his cousin's mouth. 'Sssh, sssh,' he whispered, 'you'll frighten it.'

Max, his cousin, immediately stopped moaning and groaning. 'Frighten what?' he asked as softly as he could, but Max was an American, and his quietest whisper still sounded like a shout to Peter.

'Quiet,' he hissed. 'Don't say another word. Not a word,' he warned when he saw Max opening his mouth.

'What is it?' Max mouthed the words without saying anything.

'It's a leprechaun,' Peter said quietly, and Max burst into laughter. Peter shook his head in annoyance and tried to quieten him again. Peter Casey was nearly fourteen years old; he was a tall, thin boy, with very thick, black hair that was cut in a straight line over his bright blue eyes.

'A leprechaun, a leprechaun? You must be having me on. There ain't no such thing as a leprechaun,' Max laughed, his whole body shaking with laughter. Max Gordon Nash was almost Peter's age, but he looked a lot older. He was also a lot bigger. He said that he had big bones, but Peter just said that he was fat—he had never seen anyone eat so much food so quickly in his life. Max's hair and eyebrows were fine and pale, and his eyes were a very pale grey.

Peter held both hands over Max's mouth this time until he quietened down. 'I don't care whether you believe me or not. But if you just pop your head over that bush and look down along the river bank, you'll see a leprechaun. A real, live, genuine, leprechaun—one of the Little People. Look,' he said.

Max got to his feet and rubbed the grass off his clothes. He wasn't sure whether he believed Peter or not, and he certainly didn't want to head back to his aunt's and have everyone told that he had been tricked into looking for a leprechaun. But Peter did look very serious. So, he risked a quick glance over the hedge, across the field and down towards the river—and stopped dead.

There was a leprechaun down on the river bank; a small, dark-skinned man, with a black three-cornered hat and shiny, big-buckled shoes. He had a string tied to his big toe. Max turned back to Peter, his eyes dancing. 'It's a lepre—!' he began but then realised that he was shouting and finished in a whisper, 'it's a leprechaun. What are we going to do?'

Now, everyone in Erin knows what to do when you see a leprechaun, and Peter had been told many times by his grandmother what he should do. 'The first thing we do is to make sure that we don't take our eyes off him for one second—otherwise he'll be gone.'

'O.K.' Max nodded, turning around and staring hard at the small man.

'Then we must capture him.'

Max suddenly looked doubtful. 'Capture him? Won't that be dangerous?'

'Of course,' Peter said with a grin, 'but if we can capture him, and hold him for a little while, without letting him go, we should be able to make him tell us where he keeps his crock of gold.'

Max nodded suddenly. 'Yeah, that's right. Leprechauns are supposed to keep a crock of gold hidden...' he paused and thought about it, 'or is that at the end of a rainbow?'

'Both,' Peter said impatiently. 'Now listen, here's what we'll do...' There was a sudden rustling in the grass and both boys fell silent. The rustling came closer and closer... and then a shaggy brown head popped out and licked Max's bare leg. He gave a terrified squeak and almost fell on top of Peter with fright.

'Tom-Tom, Tom-Tom, don't be so bold,' Peter scolded the dog. 'Now where have you been, eh? Off chasing rabbits, I suppose.' The dog thumped his tail on the ground happily, raising a little cloud of dust. 'You'll have to be quiet now Tom-Tom; Max and I are going to try and catch a leprechaun. He's over there beneath that tree on the river bank. We think he might be fishing.'

Tom-Tom gave a groaning sort of bark; that could only be Seamus Ban, the leprechaun.

Peter turned back to his cousin. 'Now, here's what we'll do. You creep around on that side and then hide behind that large thorn bush, and wait for me to get into position. Tom-Tom and I will go around by this side and come up to him on the far side. When you see me get very close to him, you can creep right up behind him. Then I'll speak to him. He'll probably jump then and try to run away, but you'll be behind him to stop that won't you? Won't you?' Peter asked again, when Max didn't seem to be too sure.

'Oh, yeah,yeah, of course. I'll be there,' Max promised.

Peter nodded. 'Right, off you go then.' He knelt down on the ground and watched Max run across the field and into the trees and bushes that grew along the river bank. He saw the American boy's bright red windcheater jacket moving through the trees, and he almost kicked himself for not spotting it first, but it was too late now. If the leprechaun were to wake up now, he would spot the bright red colour. However, Max got into position without any mishap, and the leprechaun was still sleeping on the river bank.

Peter set off with Tom-Tom running at his heels. He doubled back along the path, so as to come onto the river path much further upstream. Luckily, there was no one else on the path—it was more of a track, really—and he was able to make his way down to the leprechaun's position without disturbing the little man. The boy could feel his heart hammering now, and there was a fluttery, ticklish feeling in his stomach; after all, it wasn't every day you got to meet a leprechaun.

Peter Casey took a deep breath and walked right up to the figure. He coughed, and was about to speak, when the little man leaped straight up, did a tumble while still in the air and was off and running before his feet had even touched the ground!

Unfortunately, he had forgotten about the string tied around his big toe. It caught on a branch, and whipped his leg out from under him in mid-stride, dropping him to the ground with a thump. And before he could move Max knelt on the ground beside him and grabbed his arms.

The leprechaun looked at the American's wide face with his small, hard eyes. 'I am never going fishing again,' he said, but the only one who knew what he meant was Tom-Tom. The small man glared at Max. 'And just what do you want?' he demanded angrily.

'Well, eh... well...' Max looked up at Peter. 'What do we want?' he asked.

Peter knelt on the ground beside the leprechaun. 'We have you now, Mr Leprechaun, and we won't let you go until you tell us where your crock of gold is.'

Seamus Ban laughed, a merry little chuckle. 'I will not.'

'Well then, we won't let you go. In fact we'll just bring you home with us, and see what the grown-ups have to say about all of this. They will make you tell us.'

The leprechaun laughed again. 'There are only two things wrong with that,' he said. 'First, you must remember that not every human adult can see us—only a few can; and secondly, if they do find out from me where my treasure is—what makes you so sure that they're going to tell you, eh?'

The two boys thought about that for a few moments, and at last Max said, 'He might be right.'

Peter nodded glumly. 'He might. Or it might be a trick, just to try and make us let him go. Granny told me a lot of stories about the Little People and their tricky ways.'

'Well, what are you going to do then?' Max asked, looking across at Peter.

'Hold on, let me think for a few minutes,' Peter said, thinking back on all the fairy stories he had been told as a child. There must be something... 'Hush, Tom-Tom, hush,' Peter snapped as the dog began to bark furiously.

But what the boys didn't know was that Tom-Tom was talking to the leprechaun.

'I've got an idea,' Tom-Tom said quickly. 'No, don't say a word, just listen. Why don't you pretend to tell them where the gold is, and when they go to look for it, you can make your escape?'

'I've got an idea,' Peter said. 'A leprechaun cannot lie to us; he might not tell us the full truth, but he cannot tell us a direct lie. So all we have to do is to ask him different questions and we should be able to find out that way.'

Max looked doubtful. 'How do you know a leprechaun cannot lie?' he asked.

'Because they cannot,' Peter said.

'We do not tell lies,' Seamus Ban said indignantly. 'We are not like humans.'

'All right then,' Peter said, 'I'll start.' He looked at the little man. 'Is your treasure nearby?'

Seamus Ban looked very unhappy, but at last he said, 'It's not too far away from here.'

'Is it in the forest?' Peter asked.

'No,' Seamus Ban shook his head.

'Buried in the fields?'

The leprechaun shook his head again.

'In the river?' Max asked.

'No, not in the river.'

Peter sat back and thought about it again. The treasure wasn't in the forest, or in the fields or in the river... well, that left only one place. 'Is your treasure buried on the beach?'

The leprechaun said nothing for a long time, but at last he nodded his head slightly.

'Is it?' Max demanded loudly.

Again Seamus Ban nodded. 'Yes, it's buried on the beach

'Where on the beach?' the American boy asked.

'Down and in amongst the sand dunes...' the leprechaun began.

Peter raised his hand and said, 'I think it would be better if you showed us—that way no mistakes can be made.'

'If I lead you to my treasure, will you let me go?' Seamus Ban asked.

'Of course,' Peter said.

'Promise?' The leprechaun asked.

'I promise,' Peter said.

Peter and Max each took one of the leprechaun's arms and together, all three set off towards the beach, with Tom-Tom trotting along behind, giving short, sharp little barks.

But what the boys didn't know was that the dog had a plan.

They quickly smelt the sharp smell of the sea, and soon the grassy fields began to show patches of golden sand. Then the grass itself changed, from being soft and short to become long and sharp. The leprechaun was leading the two boys up the first of the sand dunes, when Max slipped and cut his hand on the ragged blades of grass. He sucked in his breath and then stopped to wind his handkerchief around the cut.

'Why is the grass so sharp?' he demanded angrily.

'It's called "bent grass",' Seamus Ban said, 'it's very strong and its roots are so tangled up that they help to keep the sand dunes together, and stop them spreading inland. The grass has to be tough to withstand the constant battering of the wind and sea.'

Max nodded glumly. 'It still hurts,' he said.

They trudged up and over the sand dune and down the other side, and then they were on the beach itself. It stretched for miles in either direction, low rounded sand dunes rising and falling like waves.

'This way,' the leprechaun said and led them down the beach. At last he stopped beside a sand dune that looked no different from any other. 'It's here,' he said quietly.

'The treasure is here?' Max asked. 'How do we know you're not tricking us?' he demanded.

'A leprechaun will never lie,' Peter said. 'If he says it's here, then it's here.' He turned to look at the little man. 'How deep is it?'

Seamus Ban shrugged. 'Four or five feet,' he said. 'You'll need shovels and spades.' He looked up at the two boys. 'Now that I've brought you to my treasure, are you going to let me go?'

'I don't think we should until we actually have the crock of gold in our hands,' Max said.

'But you promised me...' Seamus Ban said.

Peter nodded. 'We did promise to let him go if he brought us to his treasure,' he said. He let go of the leprechaun's arm. 'Thank you very much,' he said.

Max reluctantly let the little man's arm go, and nodded his thanks, and then both boys watched the small figure go scampering quickly up over the sand dunes and disappear into the tall sharp grass.

When he was gone, Peter turned to Max. 'Now, you stay here, and I'll go and get the shovels.'

'What?' Max asked, in a surprised voice. 'Stay here on my own? What do I do if he comes back with some of his friends?' he asked. 'They might drag me off to some fairy land, and I'll only be allowed to go free in a hundred years' time. No,' he shook his head, 'I'm not staying here on my own.'

'But it's the middle of the day,' Peter said. 'He won't be back.'

'He might, and I don't want to be here if he does. I'm going with you.'

'How are we going to mark this sand dune then?' Peter asked. 'Look,' he pointed up and down the beach. 'They all look alike from here; unless we leave some marker, we might not be able to find this place again.'

'How about leaving my windcheater?' Max suggested, and then he had another idea. 'How about leaving Tom-Tom here to mind it? Will he stay on his own?' he asked.

Peter nodded. 'Of course he will. Tom-Tom is a highly trained dog. That's what we'll do then.' Peter knelt in the sand and took Tom-Tom's narrow face in both his hands and stared into his large brown eyes. 'Stay, Tom-Tom, stay.' He stood up and began to back away, still looking into the dog's eyes. 'Stay.' He looked over at his cousin. 'Give me your jacket.' Max quickly pulled his arms free and handed it to Peter. He threw it at the dog's feet and Tom-Tom immediately lay down on it, with his head resting on his paws. Peter turned to his cousin. 'Come on then, let's go and get those shovels.'

Tom-Tom watched the two boys run down the beach and up over the sand dunes and then he laughed, a sort of deep chuffing sound deep in his chest. He picked up the red windcheater in his teeth and ran far down the beach, and then he dropped it on the sand before another dune and lay down with his head resting on it, exactly as he had been before. He laughed quietly to himself, waiting for the boys to return.

Peter and Max could never understand how they didn't find the treasure. They spent the rest of that summer holiday digging up the sand dune and those on either side of it, and of course, they found nothing. But it was Tom-Tom's way of thanking the leprechaun for saving his life.

The Ant

An Ant doesn't look like very much, and it is so small you might even walk on it without noticing. But the next time you are out walking, be careful, and watch where you walk, and try not to step on any of the tiny creatures. You never know when an ant might be able to help you.

This is a story about the time a poor farmer in the west of Ireland helped an ant...

Martin Newman put his hands on his hips, turned and looked back across the fields. Although he had been working since sunrise, and it was now well into the afternoon, he was only half finished. The field was full of long raised lines of earth, and each line had thick green plants growing up out of them. They were potatoes. On one side of the field, the plants lay on their sides and pale golden-brown potatoes lay in neat piles on the brown earth.

Martin rubbed his hands together, brushing off the heavy clay and tried to guess how long it would take him to finish the potato picking. He was a tall, thin young man, with thin black hair and dark sunburnt skin. His eyes were the same colour as the sky — pale blue. And now his eyes were squinting against the glare of the sun as he glanced up into the heavens. He guessed that it was about three or four o'clock in the afternoon, and then he looked back at the field again. He didn't think he was going to get finished today — but tomorrow was market day, and the first potatoes of the season would fetch the highest prices.

The young man sighed and shook his head. He would have a quick lunch and then start again. He lifted a plastic bag off the stone wall where he had left it with his coat, and pulled out the sandwiches his wife had made for him earlier that morning. In the bottom of the bag he found that she had also slipped in an apple. Martin perched on the rough stone wall and began to eat his late lunch.

As he was eating he saw storm clouds gathering in the distance, out over the sea. Old Paddy Forrest his neighbour, had told him that there would be a storm that day, and Old Paddy was never wrong about the weather.

Martin bit into his apple with a crunch and looked over his field again. He did some working out in his head and guessed that he would have the field finished by midday tomorrow. But that would be too late — the market started early in the morning. And if it rained now, the clay would get heavy and sticky, and make his work all the more difficult. He finished the apple and dropped the core by his feet, although he carefully bundled up the plastic his sandwiches had been wrapped in and put it back into his bag. Martin knew the apple would rot back into the ground, but the plastic would not.

'Back to work,' he sighed and trudged across the field to continue pulling up the potato plants and shaking the potatoes free from the roots.

Martin Newman worked as hard as he could for the rest of the afternoon. He would stop every now and again and straighten up and look back over his shoulder at the storm clouds which were much nearer now. Soon the sun was swallowed up behind them, and a cold wind blew across the field, making the young man shiver. The storm rolled in quickly — far more quickly than he had thought it would — and he only had a few more rows to pick when it began to rain.

A single drop fell first, splattering onto the green plant in his hand, little drops of silver water shooting off in all directions. Then another drop struck his face, running ice-

cold down his cheek. Another drop hit him on the back of
the neck and trickled down the collar of his shirt. And then
it looked as if someone had turned on a tap — the water
came down in a solid sheet. Martin turned up the collar of
his shirt and ran for cover.

He reached the stone wall and jumped straight over it,
and then he huddled down on the far side. Because the
wind was blowing in from the sea, the rain was also falling
in that direction and he was quite dry where he was in the
shadow of the wall. He remembered his bag and coat then
which were still up on the wall and he reached up with
one hand to pull them down. His coat was already soaking

wet, but he draped it over his shoulders, brought his knees up to his chest and folded his arms around them. He would head for home when the rain eased off a little.

There was nothing for him to do, so the young man leaned back against the wall, feeling the cold stones poke into his back, and watched the rain fall. He watched it hit the hard earth and bounce, until it looked as if there was a fine haze lying a few inches off the ground. And then a little stream of water wriggled its way out from under the stones of the wall, and twisted and curled its way past his feet. The water was coming from his field, and soon began to carry along small leaves and twigs. However, as the rain grew heavier and heavier, larger pieces of wood and small clumps of earth wound their way past Martin's boots.

And then something white was carried down on the water. It was the apple core that Martin had dropped on the ground — and perched on the back of the apple was a small black ant. The apple tumbled over and stuck, and the ant was caught under the little stream of water. Martin saw its long feelers waving about, and its legs struggling to reach the surface. But just as it managed to climb up onto the top of the apple again, a twig swept down and knocked the little creature off into the water.

Without thinking Martin reached out and scooped the little ant up in the palm of his hand. He brought his head close to his hand to look at the ant and then gently blew on it, drying it off. Soon its feelers, which had become stuck to its body, were waving in the air again, and it walked across Martin's hand and seemed to stare him straight in the eye.

'There you are now, little fellow,' Martin said. 'That will teach you to go out when it's raining. But what are we going to do with you, eh?' he asked. He looked around for some place to put the ant. 'I'll leave you here,' he decided, 'you should be safe enough.'

Martin brought his hand close to the stone wall, and gently eased the little ant off his palm with a finger. The small creature scuttled up onto the wall and disappeared into a crack in the stones. The young man glanced up into the sky — but it was still dark with heavy grey storm clouds, and the rain showed no sign of easing up. 'I suppose I had better head for home,' he said to himself. He sighed deeply. 'I'm never going to get those potatoes picked in time for market.' And then, pulling his coat up over his head, Martin set off at a run for home.

The rain eventually stopped close to midnight and then the clouds rolled quickly away, leaving a full moon shining pale and silver in the sky. The stars were like sharp little points of light, and, away in the distance, a single star fell slowly to earth, leaving a long ghostly trail behind it.

Martin Newman's fields were deserted, and the only noise was the trickling, dripping sound of water, as it fell from leaves and bushes and soaked into the ground.

And then something moved in the centre of the field.

It looked like a shadow. A broad, flat shadow — almost like a blanket thrown on the earth. But this blanket was moving. It swept out across the field and gathered around the first of the potato plants and then there was the sound of crunching and scraping, and slowly the bush toppled over, exposing the pale potatoes beneath. Part of the shadow moved onto the next bush, and soon it too fell in a shower of earth. And then something even stranger happened. Parts of this dark shadow broke up and gathered around each potato — and the potato rose up a fraction of an inch off the ground and began to glide along! Little piles of potatoes began to form about the field, and by the time the sun came up and Martin Newman's footsteps rang along the track that led to his field, every potato plant had been dug up and all the potatoes were arranged in neat little bundles, ready to put into bags.

Martin stood by the wall, with his mouth open in astonishment. What had happened? A hundred thoughts ran through his mind. Had the fairies helped him, or was

74

it perhaps ghosts, or had he really done all the work yesterday and just forgotten about it?

The young man shook his head. He didn't know — and he didn't think he would ever know.

'Thank you,' he shouted aloud, 'whoever, whatever you are. Thank you.' So, whistling happily to himself, he hopped over the wall and began to gather up the potatoes into thick bags.

In the next field a dark black shadow stopped when it heard the voice. Then it moved on and began to break up and it streamed into a deep hole beneath the wall, and quickly disappeared.

But if you had looked very closely at the shadow, you would have seen that it was made up out of millions of tiny black ants.

A Gift from the *Sidhe*

The fairy folk usually have no contact with human beings themselves, but sometimes they allow certain people to work for them. These people, because of their knowledge of the fairy world and its magic, are usually known as fairy doctors, or wise women. Of course, many people claimed to know about the fairy land, but few of them actually did.

One woman who really did know the Daoine Sidhe, the fairy folk and their ways, was Nano Hayes...

Noreen walked along behind the flock of sheep, driving them home down the winding country lane. She carried a long thin branch in one hand which she used to direct the slow animals. They knew their own way back to the farm by now, and usually were no trouble, and only Gabby, the old she-goat, insisted on wandering away.

It was late in the evening and the sun was low in the sky, casting long shadows across the ground. Noreen watched her shadow dance across the hard stony ground and wriggle up the side of a wall. She was only ten years old, but her shadow looked huge, and the warm golden sunlight turned her red hair to gold, while the dark brown shadow was the same colour as her eyes. Noreen spotted Gabby straying off the path and reached out and touched her back with the long branch. 'Come on Gabby, don't go wandering now, we're nearly home.'

The goat looked back over its shoulder and stared at her with its big soft eyes, and the young girl smiled. Although the goat was the only one of her charges that ever gave her any trouble, it was still her favourite. She ran her hand along its hairy back and scratched behind the short twitching ears. 'No time for playing now Gabby, I've got to get you home and get you milked.' The goat nodded its head and then obediently trotted off after the rest of the sheep.

Noreen continued driving the animals until she reached a little rise in the road, and then she stopped for a few moments, as she always did when the weather was clear. From here she could see right across the fields and down onto the beach and out over the waves to where the sun was setting. The sunsets at this time of year, just when the summer was finished and autumn was only starting, were always very beautiful.

Gabby came up and nuzzled its wet nose into Noreen's hand, and the young girl gently stroked its head. 'Look,' she whispered, 'look at the colours,' she said almost to herself, but the goat's ears picked up and twitched as if it understood what she had said.

So Noreen and Gabby stood on the high road and watched the sun sink slowly into the sea. But what they didn't see was a small square door opening in the stone wall behind them.

When the sun touched the water on the horizon it seemed to set the sea on fire. One moment the sea and sky were all pinks and purples, and the clouds were coloured orange and gold, and the next moment all the colours had deepened and there were dark shadows everywhere. The sky was now mostly red and a smoky grey colour, and the sea was all deep reds and oranges just where the sun had gone down, although further away it was a deep purple and blue.

Noreen looked down onto the beach. The warm orange sands were now dark brown, and only the white line of the waves showed her where the sea began and the beach stopped. Below her the fields had all fallen into shadow, but she could still see the white lines of the stone walls running across them, dividing them into rough squares.

Suddenly Gabby turned around and made an angry sort of sound. Noreen turned around to see what had upset the goat — and got a terrible fright. There was a small old woman standing right behind her! Noreen gave a little squeal, but the old woman smiled and raised a wrinkled hand.

'I'm sorry I frightened you,' the old woman said quickly, 'but I mean you no harm.'

Noreen's heart was still pounding, but she managed a small smile in return. 'You gave me such a fright,' she said. 'I didn't hear you come up, and I wasn't expecting to see anyone else up here.'

The woman smiled again. She was small and wrinkled, and looked very, very old, but her grey eyes were sharp and bright. 'My name is Nano Hayes,' she said.

Noreen frowned. She had heard that name before — but where? 'I'm Noreen Ní Muirthile,' she said, 'and this is Gabby,' she added, patting the goat.

Nano Hayes looked at the goat strangely. 'Yes, I've heard of Gabby,' she said. 'I've heard she gives the finest milk which makes the softest goat's cheese for miles around. Is that true?' she asked.

Noreen smiled proudly. 'It's true. I bring her up here every day where the grass is soft and sweet.'

The old woman nodded again, and then she looked at Noreen with her sharp bright eyes. She was wearing a long black shawl over her head and across her shoulders, so that only her wrinkled apple of a face was showing. She smiled again, but this time Noreen found the smile frightening. 'I would like to borrow Gabby for a while,' she said.

'Borrow her?' Noreen asked, shocked.

Nano Hayes nodded. 'For a little while,' she said.

'But you can't... I mean, I couldn't. What would my father say?' Noreen asked.

'I would explain everything to your father,' the old woman said.

Noreen shook her head. 'Well, I don't think he will lend her to you.'

Nano Hayes smiled again. 'Oh, but he will lend her to me.'

'But what do you want her for — and why Gabby? There must be hundreds of goats all over the country.'

'There are hundreds of goats,' Nano Hayes said, 'but none of them give such sweet milk, and none of their milk can be made into such lovely cheese.'

The sun had now sunk and it was that time of grey mistiness before night properly fell. Noreen shivered suddenly. 'But why do you need to borrow Gabby? We could sell you milk or cheese if you need it.' The old woman shook her head, and a slight breeze whipped up part of her dark shawl. 'No, Noreen,' she said, 'that wouldn't work. I will need Gabby for...' she paused and seemed to be thinking, 'oh, at least three months.'

'Three months!'

Nano Hayes nodded again. 'Three months, perhaps longer. I will need fresh goat's milk twice a day, every day for those three months, and I will need fresh goat's cheese at least once a week. So you see why I must have Gabby close by me.'

'But why do you need so much milk and cheese?' Noreen asked.

The old woman hesitated before answering, but at last she said, 'I need it as part of a cure...'

'A cure?' the young girl said, and then she suddenly knew where she had heard the old woman's name before. 'You're Nano Hayes, the Wise Woman,' she said excitedly.

The old woman gave a little nod.

'My father has told me about you — he said you saved his life when he was a little boy.'

Nano Hayes smiled. 'I cured a bad cold, that's all,' she said.

'He says you're a witch, and a friend of the Little People,' Noreen said quickly.

'Well, he's only half right,' Nano Hayes said quietly, 'I'm not a witch, but I am a friend of the fairy folk. And that's why I need Gabby,' she added. 'The young princess is sick, with a strange disease and no one seems to know what it is. The fairy folk have asked me to try and cure it.'

'What's wrong with her?' the young girl asked.

'I think she ate some of those brightly coloured mushrooms that you sometimes see growing wild.'

'But I thought that they were poisonous?' Noreen said.

Nano Hayes nodded. 'They are. Now, can I have Gabby please?'

'Can I come with you?' Noreen asked suddenly. 'Please?'

Nano Hayes shook her head. 'Who will bring the sheep home?' she asked, nodding towards the white sheep that were still slowly wandering down the road.

'They will find their own way home,' Noreen said, 'the road only leads to the farm. And I can pin a note to one of their backs, telling mother and father where I've gone.' She saw Nano Hayes starting to shake her head, but Noreen hurried on. 'Please, it's probably the only time I'll ever get to see the fairy lands. Anyway,' she added, 'Gabby will let no one milk her except me!'

The old woman gave a short laugh. 'Girl,' she said, 'I've milked more cows and goats than you could ever imagine, and, while I'm not a witch, I know enough magic to make that animal milk herself.' She smiled gently, her eyes sparkling. 'However, if you want to come into fairy land with me, you had better hurry up and write that note.'

Noreen quickly searched her pockets for a scrap of paper and a stub of a pencil, and then she scribbled a note to her parents, telling them what had happened, and where she was going. She felt sure they wouldn't mind, once they knew that she was going with Nano Hayes, the Wise Woman. Then the young girl ran down the road and tied the note to the back of one of the sheep with its own fleece.

When she returned to the old woman, she found that she was standing beside the rock wall just off the path. Noreen looked at the wall carefully; she passed it every day, and she had never noticed anything strange about. It looked just like any other rock wall: different sized flat stones piled up atop the other, a few feet high. It was certainly no thicker than six or eight inches.

'What are we waiting for?' she asked Nano Hayes.

The old woman touched the wall with the tips of the fingers of her right hand, and immediately a green spark jumped from them onto the stones. The green spark buzzed and crackled softly and then it raced around the wall, leaving a thin green square shape on the stones. The spark then gave a final crackle and fizzled out. Nano Hayes then touched the stones again — and a door swung back!

Noreen felt her breath catch in her throat and her heart began to pound. She bent her head and peered through the door — and got another shock: there was bright sunlight on the other side. She stepped back and looked at the wall again. But it still looked like the same old wall; over it she could make out the dim shapes of the fields and rising in the distance the mountains. Yet, through the door was a bright sunlit field, with tiny red and blue star-shaped flowers scattered on the pale green grass. She looked across at Nano Hayes, and the old woman smiled.

'Fairyland,' she said, and then she bent over and stepped through into the other world.

Noreen took another look, and then she glanced over her shoulder down over the fields and onto the beach, just to make sure that they were still there. And then, holding tightly onto Gabby's long hair, she stepped into fairyland...
...And found that she didn't feel any different. She had expected to feel a tingling or a chill or maybe even a shiver run up her back, but she felt nothing — except a lot warmer. Noreen turned and looked at the wall — and found she was facing another wall, exactly the same as the one she had left in her own world, except that through this door she could see the darkened beach and the blue-black sea back in Erin.

Nano Hayes then took her by the arm and led her across the field and out onto a thin white path that ran in a straight line off into the distance.

'This is fairyland,' Nano Hayes said quietly, 'the Otherworld, the Land of the *Sidhe*. Now, before we meet anyone, you must listen to me very carefully, and you must always do as I tell you — otherwise you will become trapped here, and even I will not be able to help you then. Do you understand?'

Noreen nodded without saying a word.

'Good. Now, the first thing to remember is that you must neither eat nor drink anything. If you are offered anything to eat you must say that you like plenty of salt with your food. The fairy folk cannot bear to have salt near them, and that will make sure that they will offer you nothing else. If you are offered any drink, you must ask for it in an iron cup. Again, the fairy folk cannot bear to have iron near them.'

'What will I eat then?' Noreen asked.

Nano Hayes smiled. 'It's a funny thing, but in fairyland you don't feel hungry, and time is different here. You might spend a day here, but find that a week, or a month, or even a year has passed back in our world.' She stopped and looked at the girl. 'It's not too late to turn back.'

Noreen shook her head. 'No, I won't turn back.'

Nano Hayes smiled again and then quickened her step and hurried down the road, with the young girl by her side, and Gabby trotting along behind.

Nano Hayes told Noreen stories about the fairy land, and about her adventures in it, with the Little People, the fairy folk, the leprechauns, the cluricauns, the Shining Ones, and Banshees, and the terrible Phookas, the demon horses. As they were walking down the track, the old woman also pointed out the strange trees and flowers of the Otherworld, trees and flowers that grew nowhere else. They passed through a grove of metal trees. The tree trunks and branches were silver, and the leaves were gold, and they were polished like mirrors. They crossed a bridge of glass, that made Noreen dizzy when she looked down into the foaming river beneath. Nano Hayes led her beneath tall rocks that seemed to turn ever so slowly to stare at them, and the girl thought she heard them rumbling quietly together. They passed stones which rolled along beside them for a while, and bushes which trembled and shivered as they walked by.

But there were no animals; no birds flew in the sky, no insects crawled on the ground or basked in the sun, and no sheep or cows walked around the fields. And when Noreen asked Nano Hayes about this, all the old woman would say was, 'They are sleeping. The fairy beasts only come forth at night. They are creatures of the dark. Why is it that Phookas, the fairy horses, are only heard and seen at night, and why is it that fairy cows only come out and graze at night?'

Noreen shook her head and said she didn't know.

'Because at night the doors between the fairy lands and our world are fully opened and the creatures from this place are able to wander through.'

'Where are these doors?' Noreen asked in a whisper.

'Usually in the sides of fairy forts,' Nano Hayes said. 'But some of the beasts can come up out of the water from the Land Beneath the Waves, which is another part of fairyland.'

'But what about the door you made?' the girl asked.

'I was given that power by the fairy folk themselves,' Nano Hayes said. 'I can come and go into the Otherworld whenever I please.' Nano Hayes stopped suddenly and pointed. 'Look — there.' She was pointing towards a collection of low mounds that rose like hills in the distance.

'It looks like a town,' Noreen said, 'what is it called?'

'It's called the Fort,' the old woman said. 'It's not really a town, it's more a collection of houses where the fairy folk can stay whenever there is a special gathering.'

'Where do the fairy folk live?' Noreen asked.

Nano Hayes smiled. 'We have been passing their houses ever since we came into this world. Well, they're not really the sort of houses you or I are used to. Most of them live in special holes in the ground or caves that blend in perfectly with the landscape. They think that anything that interferes with the way nature looks is ugly.'

Noreen thought about it and then nodded her head. 'I think so too,' she said, and even Gabby nodded her shaggy head also.

They had come quite close to the Fort now, but it still took Noreen a few moments to make out the shapes. The houses were all small and rounded, more like little mounds than anything else, and it wasn't until she was quite close to them did she see that they were actually set into the ground, and there were steps leading down to their doors. Nano Hayes laughed at her confusion. 'What you are looking at are the roofs of the buildings, the rest of the house is below ground.'

As they were passing the first building, the door opened and someone walked up the steps and out onto the 'street'. The young girl stopped and stared in amazement at the figure. It too stopped and looked from her to Nano Hayes and smiled.

'Is this her first time?' he asked, in a bright, high voice.

The old woman nodded. 'She's never seen a leprechaun before.'

Noreen remembered her manners then and smiled at the small man in the bright green coat, red stockings, large hat and shiny black shoes with the huge buckles. 'Hello. I'm sorry for staring at you, but...'

The small man laughed. 'Oh, there's no need to be sorry. I remember staring myself the first time I saw one of the Big Folk.' He tipped his hat and gave a little bow, and then hurried off.

The young girl turned to Nano Hayes. 'Who are the Big Folk?' she asked.

'We are,' Nano Hayes said with a smile. 'Come on now, we must hurry.'

The old woman led Noreen through the maze of low humps that were the fairy folk's houses, and then stopped outside a hump that looked no different from any of the others. 'The Palace,' she said.

The girl looked at it in surprise. '*This?*' she said. She had expected something bigger, grander.

Nano Hayes looked back at her in surprise. 'Oh, you must never judge anything by its appearance,' she said, starting down the steps that led to a simple arched door. She paused before the door and looked back. 'Will Gabby come down the steps?'

'Of course,' Noreen said, and led the goat down the few steps to the doorway.

Nano Hayes knocked softly on the door with a small wrinkled hand. It was opened almost immediately by a tall, thin young girl, with pale green skin and fine green hair. Her eyes were wide and slightly slanted and were the colour of grass. She bowed when she saw Nano Hayes and stepped aside.

The old woman hurried through the open door, with Noreen and the goat following. But once inside the girl stopped in astonishment. Instead of the small hallway she had been expecting, she found she was in a huge circular room that stretched far into the distance. There were pillars everywhere and the walls were covered with rich hanging drapes. There was a carpet on the floor that was so thick she could actually feel herself sink slowly into it. She

turned and found the strange fairy girl staring at her, but Noreen found her just a little frightening, and she hurried off after Nano Hayes.

They seemed to be walking for a very long time. The palace was huge and stretched off in every direction. Everywhere Noreen looked she saw corridors disappearing into the distance, and there were wide staircases winding up for floor after floor. The palace itself was very beautiful. The walls — where they were not covered with tapestries — seemed to be made of white marble, and every door was made of solid gold. The doors were also covered with thousands of tiny pictures, which Nano Hayes said told the story of the fairy folk and how they came to the land of Erin. All the corridors seemed to have at least one tiny wind chime hanging up somewhere, which tinkled and tingled softly all the time, so that the palace was always full of very gentle music.

At last Nano Hayes stopped before a tall double door. Unlike the others this door was just made of some shiny black material which Noreen thought looked like polished coal, but which Nano Hayes called jet. There was a very simple celtic-style design running all around the edge of the two doors and the two handles were each made in an old Irish design.

The old woman put her hand on the doors, but before she opened them, she looked back at Noreen. 'Remember, eat nothing, drink nothing, and do as I say.' The girl had a chance to nod once before Nano Hayes threw the doors open and walked in.

After the beauty of the rest of the palace, Noreen had expected the room to be something extra special, and she was almost disappointed to find that it was a small, simple bedroom, with a single bed set against the wall, and a low table beside it. There was nothing else in the room, and the only other person there was someone in the bed.

Nano Hayes hurried over to the bed and looked down. She smiled gently and settled the silken sheets and then looked over at the girl. 'Will you milk Gabby for me, please? You can use the jug on the table.'

While Noreen took the jug and sat down crosslegged on the thickly carpeted floor, Nano Hayes gently woke the young girl sleeping in the bed. She sat up, her golden eyes sleepy and her pale golden hair all mussed. The tiny girl — she was much smaller than Noreen — looked at the goat and then at the human girl and turned to Nano Hayes.

'Is that a goat?' she asked. Her voice was soft and gentle, very musical and sweet and almost like a whisper.

The old woman nodded. 'Aye, that's Gabby the goat. And that is her keeper and minder, Noreen. She is going to start milking the goat in a moment, and then you will have fresh goat's milk. I want you to drink it all down,' she added.

'I'm hungry,' the golden-haired girl said, 'I want something more than goat's milk.'

'Well, goat's milk is all you are going to get,' Nano Hayes said sternly. She turned back to Noreen. 'This is Shee, princess of this land, and in a hundred years or so she might even be queen — if she does what she is supposed to do, and takes her medicine.'

'The medicine is horrible,' Shee interrupted.

'As you can see,' Nano Hayes continued, ignoring the fairy-child, 'she is not very well behaved, although she is around you own age, I think.' She then nodded at Gabby. 'You can start milking now.'

Noreen began to milk the goat, and thin streams of pale yellow-white liquid shot out and plinked into the jug she had placed on the floor, while Gabby stood patiently, without moving. When the jug was full, Nano Hayes came over and Noreen handed it up to her. The old woman tasted the steaming warm milk and nodded. 'That's lovely.'

She carried it back over to the bed and offered it to Shee. 'Drink this,' she said, 'it will help to make you well again.'

But Shee just folded her arms and shook her head. 'I will not drink that awful stuff,' she snapped.

Nano Hayes was just about to speak when the door opened and two of the most beautiful people Noreen had ever seen entered the room. They must be the king and queen, she thought. They were almost identical, both were very tall, with silver-gold hair, long thin faces, with pointed chins, and slightly slanting eyes. Their fingers also seemed to be very long. They were dressed in gauzy robes of purest silk, and had simple crowns on their heads that seemed to be made of glass and the king wore a sword made from the same material.

When they spoke their voices were so beautiful that they seemed to be singing. 'I hope you are not being difficult again, Shee,' the man said.

'I am not,' Shee said in a sullen voice. 'But she wants me to drink that awful stuff.'

'If Nano Hayes wants you to drink something then I think you had better drink it.' The king's voice hardened. 'Now, I have told you before, Shee, Nano Hayes has come a long way just to help you. She has gone to a lot of trouble to find fresh goat's milk and I can only hope that you will do as she says!'

'But why do I have to drink that stuff?' Shee asked.

'Because you ate something you shouldn't have,' Nano Hayes said quickly, 'because that poisoned you, and because if you eat anything else — *anything* the poison will begin to work again, and you will die. The goat's milk will keep you alive and strong until the poison has passed from your body. Only then will you be well again.'

'Shee,' the queen said in a quiet voice, 'you will do as Nano Hayes tells you. There will be no more trouble from you,' she said in the same soft voice, but everyone heard the stern warning in it.

Shee nodded obediently.

Nano Hayes handed the steaming jug of fresh goat's milk to the tiny fairy-girl. 'Drink,' she said.

And Shee drank.

Every day for the next twelve weeks Nano Hayes, with Noreen and Gabby, would go to the fairy princess' room, and the young girl would milk the goat and Shee would drink it. Every fifth day, the old woman would have Noreen keep some of the goat's milk, and this she handed over to one of the tall beautiful people, the *Daoine Sidhe*. They would come back to her a little while later with a pat of fresh goat's cheese, made from the milk. Shee liked this even less than the milk but Nano Hayes made her eat it.

During the day, Gabby was allowed to wander through the fields of fairyland, eating the fresh, sweet grass and drinking the crystal clear, ice-cold water. Her milk grew thicker and lovelier every day.

While the goat fed, Nano Hayes would take Noreen and show her the various sights of the strange land. She showed her the ice palaces of the northern fairy folk, which were sparklingly beautiful. They visited *Tír na nÓg*, the Land of Youth, in the wide Western Ocean, where no one ever aged, and where creatures out of myth and legend still roamed — dragons, griffins, huge wolves, long-toothed tigers, and unicorns. Nano Hayes brought her to *Tír Faoi Thoinn*, the Land Beneath the Waves, home of Manannan, the Lord of the Sea. Noreen saw palaces of coral and hardened sand, carpets of woven seaweed and moss. There were mermaids there also, and giant sea-horses and huge many-armed squid, gentle-eyed dolphins, and many-toothed whales.

But the old woman always made sure that they were back in the Fort by the time night fell, because then the Fairy Host rode out on their smoky-eyed horses, and even Nano Hayes didn't want to meet them.

Noreen asked why they rode out into the human world by night.

The old wise woman smiled sadly. 'It reminds them that they once ruled our world, and sometimes they take young men or women and bring them back here to work as servants.'

'Do they take children?' Noreen asked in a whisper.

Nano Hayes nodded. 'Sometimes; if they see a very beautiful baby they might take it and leave one of their own behind.'

'But the fairy folk are so beautiful,' the girl said, 'why should they want to take beautiful human babies?'

'Because fairy babies are very ugly indeed, and the fairy folk only love beautiful things.'

So the weeks passed, and day by day Shee began to look better. A little colour came into her cheeks and her hair took on a sheen and even her pale eyes brightened. Her temper and manners improved and she took the goat's milk and cheese with no arguments. And, by the time the twelve weeks were up, she was completely recovered.

Nano Hayes stood beside her bed on the morning of the last day, and handed the princess her last drink of goat's milk. Shee took it without a word and drank it down in one gulp. She made a face. 'I still think it tastes terrible,' she said.

The old woman smiled. 'I know. But it has saved your life.'

Shee nodded, and then she said. 'Can I get up now?'

'You can get up,' Nano Hayes said, and then she turned as the door opened and the king and queen entered the room. 'Your daughter is cured,' the old woman said, 'but you must warn her never to eat any wild mushrooms ever again.'

'I won't,' Shee promised.

The king smiled. 'I think she has learned her lesson.' He then looked from the old woman to Noreen. 'I know you wish to return to your own world,' he said with a smile, 'but we are preparing a feast in your honour — will you stay and eat with us?'

Noreen glanced at the old woman before turning to the king. 'I would very much like to,' she said, 'but I am afraid that I like plenty of salt on my food, and I only drink out of iron cups and eat off iron plates.'

The king laughed softly. 'I see Nano Hayes has taught you well.' He looked over at the old woman. 'Will she be the next wise woman?' he asked.

'She might be,' was all she would say, and then, bowing to the king and queen, Nano Hayes took Noreen by the hand and walked out of the door. Gabby gave a final bleat to the fairy folk and hurried after her, glad to be going home.

When Noreen stepped through the door in the stone wall, she found it was evening, and, what was even more surprising, she found that she could see her herd of sheep slowly wandering down the road. The old woman bent and kissed her cheek. 'I told you time was different in fairyland,' she said, and then stepped back into the wall and closed the door behind her.

Noreen stood looking at it for a few moments before setting off at a run after her sheep. And, as she suspected, she found her note still tied to the back of one of them. Although she had spent three months in fairyland, only a few minutes had passed in her own world. She had heard something jangling in her pocket as she ran, and when she looked, she found a small red cloth purse. Inside there were two silver coins.

But Noreen knew what it was; it was a fairy purse, and as long as she spent only one of those coins, and then closed the purse, when she would open it again she would find two. It was a purse that would never empty — a gift from the *Sidhe*.

Many years later, when Noreen had almost — but not quite — forgotten about her trip to the Otherworld, the old woman came to visit her again. Nano Hayes told her that she was leaving this world and going into the Sidhe world for the rest of her days, and the fairy folk needed a new wise woman.

And the king and queen, and especially Princess Shee, asked for Noreen to become the new wise woman — which she did. But that is another story.

The Cricket's Tale

If you live in the country, you will be used to the sound of a cricket singing away to himself behind the fire. The heat attracts them, and they usually begin rasping when the house falls quiet.

It is usually considered lucky to have a cricket living in the house, because crickets are supposed to be magical creatures and not really from this world. They are supposed to live to a great age and to know all the secrets of the animal world...

Paul woke with a start, and for a moment he didn't know where he was. A book dropped from his hand and hit the floor with a bang and he suddenly remembered: he was sitting before the huge open fireplace in Granny Pringle's cottage. He looked at the large-faced old clock hanging on the dark wall above the fireplace — half past ten! Where were his parents and Gran?

Paul Donovan and his parents were spending a month of their holidays in the north of Ireland with his father's mother, Mrs Pringle. Paul, a small, pale-haired, grey-eyed, eleven-year-old, came from Melbourne, in Australia, and this was his first visit to his father's home country.

Paul had never met his Grandmother before — nor had his own mother for that matter. Paul's father had emigrated to Australia nearly fifteen years ago and had settled there and married. But now that he was back, all the relations — and there seemed to be hundreds — had to meet Patrick Donovan again. From the moment they arrived, they seemed to spend more time just travelling from one small town to another, or from farm to farm, meeting cousins, second-cousins, third-cousins, uncles, aunts, god-mothers and goodness knows who else.

They were supposed to be going out tonight to some party that was being held in their honour, but Paul, who had spent the day roaming over the Giant's Causeway, had said that he was very tired, and would prefer to stay at home. His parents had agreed and had headed off to the party with his grandmother, after making him promise that he wouldn't go near the huge open fireplace.

As soon as they had gone, Paul had dragged over one of the big soft chairs in front of the fire and curled up on it with a book of Irish folk and fairy tales which his father had bought him at Dublin Airport.

And then he heard the cricket.

Paul smiled when he heard it; it reminded him of home, and somehow it made the big old house seem just a little bit less lonely. Paul opened the book of fairy tales and began to read...

...And now he was awake. He had fallen asleep while reading about Fionn, his almost-human dog, Bran, and the rest of the knights of the Fianna, and he had been having a strange half-dream when he had woken up. It was the type of dream where he knew that he was dreaming but wasn't able to wake up. It wasn't even a frightening dream — just strange.

Paul wondered what had wakened him. He listened carefully, but the house was very quiet — very quiet indeed. And then he realised that the old clock above the fireplace had stopped. He looked at his wristwatch — it was three minutes to twelve, not half past ten!

The cricket in the fireplace rasped again and the sudden noise set his heart pounding. He tried to laugh, but his own voice sounded very lost in the silence. 'That gave me a bit of a fright,' he said, more to hear the sound of his voice than anything else.

The cricket 'sang' again, its long hind legs rasping together. The sound was coming from somewhere down beside the fire, and the noise it made even sounded like the word cricket.

'Krik-it, krik-it.'

Paul stretched and yawned. That was probably what had awoken him, the cricket *'krikiting'* to himself. And then he suddenly thought of something. He picked up the book of folk tales off the floor and looked at the contents — but what he was looking for wasn't there, so he turned to the back to the index, which was an alphabetical list of all the subjects which were in the book and the pages they were on. He ran a finger down the 'Cs' — and yes, there it was, *Crickets in Irish Folklore*, page 185. He thumbed through the book looking for the page.

'One hundred and eighty, eighty-one, eighty-two, eighty-three, eighty-four... here it is, one hundred and eighty-five,' Paul said aloud. *'Crickets and Irish country lore. It is always lucky to have a cricket singing in the hearth,'* he read. He wondered what a hearth was for a moment, and then he realised it must be the fireplace. He continued reading. *'Because the fairy folk have very sensitive hearing they cannot bear to come near a cricket — and it keeps them away from the house. It is always advisable to have a cricket in a house where there is a new-born baby.'* Paul stopped reading and thought about it. That would be to stop the fairy folk from swapping the human baby with one of their own ugly children. He shook his head. He didn't think crickets were so important!

The cricket was still singing in the hearth, so he got down on his hands and knees and stared in behind the fire, looking for the small insect. Although the fire had died down to red and black glowing coals, the heat was still strong enough to make him squint his eyes and he could feel his cheeks grow warm and then hot. He gave up looking for it after a few minutes because it got so warm. Paul got up and brushed off his hands and knees, settled back into the chair, and picked up his book — and got a shock: the cricket was perched on the cover, its long antennae waving slowly at him!

'Krik-it, krik-it,' it said.

Paul grinned. 'I was just looking for you,' he said softly, looking closely at the tiny creature. In the warm light from the fire, it looked as if it were black and red-gold.

'Krik-it, krik-it,' the insect chirped.

'Cricket, cricket to you too,' Paul said. 'I was just reading about you — apparently you're quite an important little fellow in Irish folklore.'

'Krik-it, krik-it... of course I am!'

Paul dropped the book with shock. The cricket had just spoken to him! Suddenly the small creature hopped up onto the arm of his chair, its long antennae waving furiously at him.

'Kirk-it, krik-it, you nearly squashed me!' The voice was very thin and high, and slightly rasping — and it was certainly coming from the cricket.

Paul pointed at it, his mouth opening and closing like a small fish. 'But, you're a cricket, you can't talk,' he whispered.

'Who says I can't?' the insect rasped.

'But...?' Paul said, but found he couldn't think of anything to say. Well, what do you say to a cricket? This was not happening, he told himself. He had fallen asleep in his Grandmother's kitchen, and he was dreaming all this. He pinched himself to wake up. But the pinch hurt — and he didn't wake up, which meant that he was already awake, which meant that the talking cricket must be real!

'But I've never heard a cricket talk before,' he began.

'Does that mean you've never even *heard* of a talking cricket before?' the creature demanded, with an angry krik-it.

Paul thought about it. 'Both,' he said finally.

'You're not Irish,' the insect said suddenly.

'I'm from Australia,' Paul mumbled, wondering if he were going mad.

'Krik-it, krik-it, that explains it,' the cricket said, 'it's only Irish crickets that are special, magical creatures. Your Australian insects are just common or garden crickets.'

'How are you special?' the boy wondered.

The insect's antennae waved around and around. 'How? Because we're not from this world,' it said, sounding surprised. 'Surely you knew that?'

Paul shook his head, but said nothing.

'Krik-it, krik-it, we first came to this land from the country of Tuatha De Danann,' the insect began, and then paused. 'You have heard of the Tuatha De Dannan?' it asked.

Paul nodded. 'Oh yes, I read a story about their coming to Banba...'

The cricket's antennae waved. 'Yes, that's right, we came from the magical city of Falias when the People of the Goddess sailed on the *Seeker* in search of a new land. My people hid in amongst the supplies when they were being loaded aboard.' He stopped and gave a short little bow. 'My name, by the way, is Criogar. I am the oldest and wisest cricket in all Ireland.'

'Pleased to meet you,' the boy said, 'my name is Paul Donovan.' And then he asked. 'How are you the oldest and wisest cricket in Ireland? I thought crickets only lived for a short while.'

'Ordinary crickets do,' Criogar said in his high, scratching voice, 'but I am not an ordinary cricket — I came from a magical land, which means that I too am magical. I have lived for thousands of years. I have watched all the different invaders who came to the land of Erin after the Tuatha De Dannan. I have seen all the great heroes and heroines of Irish legend. I have known all the different fairy-folk, and I know all the secrets of the animals.'

'How.' Paul asked, interested now.

'Because I speak their language,' Criogar said, sounding surprised. 'In fact,' he added in a boastful voice, 'I know most things. Ask me a question. Go on — ask me a question, any question.'

'What sort of question?' Paul asked.

'Any sort of question,' the cricket said.

Paul thought about it for a moment, and then he said, 'All right then; I was reading a story in this book about Bran, Fionn's dog...'

Criogar waved his antennae. 'I knew him well — him and his brother Sceolan too of course. Do you know they weren't real dogs? Their mother was human, but she had been changed into a dog by an evil fairy woman before they were born...'

The boy nodded impatiently. 'Yes, I know that; that's what it says in this story. But what I want to know is how did Bran die?'

'Krik-it, die? Krik-it, die? Bran didn't die. He couldn't die. He was a magical creature, and magical creatures never die.'

'Well, what happened to him then?' Paul asked.

Criogar suddenly hopped up onto the arm of the chair and then slowly and delicately walked up along Paul's sleeve onto his shoulder. The boy could feel the cricket's waving antennae brush against his cheek. When he spoke, his voice sounded very soft and feathery. 'Look into the fire, and tell me what you see,' the cricket said.

'Why?' Paul asked.

'Just do as I say,' Criogar said, and the boy obediently stared into the dying fire. At first all he saw were the thick lumps of half-burned coal, and beneath them the rich, deep red glow of the fire. A coal shifted in the grate and tiny sparks whirled up the big, wide chimney. 'Look deep into the fire,' the cricket whispered in his clicking voice.

Paul continued staring deep into the fire. Now he saw the thin covering of pale grey ash over the coal, and the little flames dancing over the surface and the faint threads of smoke drifting up the chimney. But as he continued looking, a strange thing began to happen; he thought he saw something deep in the very heart of the fire. He blinked and blinked again and then a lump of coal — black on one

side and rich red on the other — fell back, allowing him to look right into the very centre of the fire.

And he saw something move. He blinked, squeezing his eyes shut, counting to five before opening them again, but when he finally did open them, he saw the same thing. The boy found he wasn't looking at a fire any more, but at a picture of a long, low hill, covered with rich green grass and tiny flowers. Even as he watched he saw the image become clearer and clearer, until he almost felt as if he were walking down the hill with a fresh wind on his face and spots of rain brushing against his cheeks. He opened his mouth to speak, but something tickled his ear and he heard a familiar clicking voice. 'Say nothing, just watch.'

Paul said nothing and watched.

He looked around and found he was indeed standing on a sloping green hillside. Away in the distance he could see the deep blue of the sea, while at the bottom of the hill was a lake that was so blue it was almost purple. The waters of the lake were very still, and reflected the slowly moving grey-white clouds overhead. Paul heard a sound behind him and turned around. He saw a man come over the brow of the hill, with a huge shaggy dog by his side. The man was very tall, and carried a spear that was even taller than he was. He had a sharp face, and bright red hair and beard. He was wearing thick leather armour, woollen trousers and a cloak of the same material on his shoulders that was held with a beautiful gold pin at his throat.

'That is Fionn,' Criogar's voice rasped in the boy's ear.

The tall proud warrior walked slowly down the hillside, moving carefully and cautiously, watching, listening, even smelling the clean morning air. The huge wolf-hound padded along beside him. The dog was as high as Paul and looked more like a small horse than a dog. His head was long, his eyes sharp and bright and his ears were constantly twitching and turning.

'And that is Bran,' Criogar whispered. 'Don't worry,' he added, when Paul tried to move out of the way as the man and dog came very close, 'we can see them, but they cannot see us.'

Suddenly the dog stopped, his long head pointing off to one side. Fionn immediately stopped also, and then he slowly sank down into the long grass and seemed to disappear. Bran lay down on his stomach and then began to creep along the ground like a snake, moving towards a thick clump of bushes and a few small trees which lay ahead.

Meanwhile, Fionn moved quickly and quietly off to one side, hoping to get into the position towards which Bran's quarry would make.

Paul looked back at Bran. He couldn't see the dog, but he could see a sort of flattened track where the dog was creeping through the grass. When he was very close to the bushes, he stopped. The young boy was just about to ask Criogar what was going to happen, when the dog suddenly bounded up out of the grass and dashed for the bushes, barking furiously. Paul wasn't close enough to see what was happening, but he did see the bushes shaking and quivering, and even the small trees swayed from side to side as the heavy dog brushed past them. Leaves and twigs scattered in all directions and birds rose screaming and cawing up into the air.

And the something dashed out of the trees. Something small and long-legged. It was a deer, a smooth-skinned, large-eyed, long-legged red deer. It ran in a long bounding run — straight towards the hiding man.

Fionn stood up at the last moment, his long, heavy spear raised in his hand and ready to throw. The red deer came to a quivering halt for a moment, and looked over its shoulder, but Bran was very close behind her, growling and snarling. The deer gave a little half jump and then dashed straight towards Fionn!

The warrior hesitated for a moment. He didn't know what to do — the animal should be trying to run away from him, giving him a broad target for his hunting spear, instead of running straight at him. Fionn then spread his legs and gripped the spear tightly in both hands, waiting for the deer to come close. However, at the very last moment, just before Fionn lunged at it, the animal put on a burst of speed and dashed straight between his legs. The tall man stabbed down with his spear, but it was too late and all he did was to drive the broad head straight into the ground. And while he was trying to pull it out, Bran ran straight into him. The heavy animal bowled the man over, and they both went down in a tumble of human arms and dog legs.

Paul didn't know whether to cheer or laugh. He was quite pleased that the beautiful red deer had escaped — but at the same time, he didn't like to see Fionn and Bran made to look foolish, and he also knew that the deer would probably have been their dinner for the next day or two.

But suddenly Bran was up and racing after the deer, his long legs pumping, his ears flat against his head and his long tail sailing out behind. He was moving so fast that at times he almost seemed to leave the ground and sail through the air for short spaces.

Then the deer, which had slowed down a little, noticed the dog, and she began to run even harder and faster than she had done before. She dodged and weaved around bushes, her four long legs with their tiny feet sending up little spurts of dust and earth as she skidded and slipped as she turned. Bran just pounded on behind, his long legs eating up the distance, coming closer and closer with every bound he took.

The red deer was now very close to the water of the lake, but, instead of turning away, she only seemed to quicken her pace — heading straight for the water.

But Bran was almost on top of her now, and his jaws with their long yellow teeth snapped at her heels.

And then the deer ran into the lake. Water splashed everywhere as Bran followed her in, and for a moment it was impossible to see anything in the spray — but when the spray had vanished and the water settled down again, both Bran and the red deer had disappeared.

'What happened to them?' Paul whispered in

amazement. 'They couldn't have just drowned so quickly — could they? Where have they gone?' he asked.

'Krik-it sssh, krik-it,' Criogar rasped. 'Watch.'

Fionn raced down to the water's edge, calling the dog's name. He splashed into the shallows and began to probe ahead of him with his spear, wondering if the ground fell away sharply, as it sometimes did with inland lakes. Perhaps Bran had just run out into the water and then fallen down. But if that was the case, where was the body? And anyway, Bran was a magical animal, he wouldn't — *couldn't* — drown so easily.

Fionn continued testing the depth of the water with his spear, moving out further and further all the time — but the ground continued to slope away gently. It was a mystery. He was just about to wade back to shore to take off his armour and heavy clothes and go back to swim in the deeper water and look for Bran when he noticed a strange disturbance out in the centre of the lake.

It was as if a huge stone had been dropped into the water. There was a ripple, a huge round ripple that quickly spread out across the surface of the small lake, making little waves that lapped at the warrior's feet. Then the very centre of the circling ripple began to bubble and boil, and the water turned white and frothing.

The tall warrior then knew that there was magic about and quickly stepped away from the lakeside. He could fight giants and monsters, even whole armies and terrible demons — but he couldn't fight magic. Even so he kept a tight hold on his spear, ready to throw.

A figure began to rise far out in the centre of the lake — a tall, thin, beautifully-dressed, very lovely woman. Paul immediately knew that she was a fairy woman — and he also knew that she had been the red deer, because of the colour of her skin and her large soft eyes.

'Where is my dog?' Fionn demanded angrily, and though he wasn't speaking English, Paul could understand him.

'Asleep,' the fairy woman said, with a cruel smile.

'Give him back to me, or else…'

'Or else what, Fionn, son of Cumhal, what will you do? Even the druid's magic is not strong enough to bring your dog back. No,' she shook her head, her long hair waving from side to side, 'your dog chased me, and now he is trapped here for a thousand years and more.'

'Let him go,' Fionn said again, his voice growing angry.

'No,' the fairy woman said simply.

And then Fionn suddenly drew back his arm and threw his spear. It sped through the air, its broad copper head winking in the sunlight, straight towards the fairy woman. There was a splash and then a long spout of water, as thick and as twisting as a rope, came shooting up out of the lake and wrapped itself around the spear and quickly dragged it down into the depths.

The fairy woman smiled again. 'There is nothing you can do Fionn, Bran is mine...'

'Kirk-it, krik-it, and there wasn't,' Criogar said into Paul's ear. 'Fionn tried everything he could — but the fairy woman's magic was stronger, and nothing would bring Bran back. He was trapped there, and there he remains. But as time went by, the story changed, as all stories do with time, and some people said that Fionn himself had killed Bran to stop him killing a deer which was really his own wife, but changed by magic. But I don't believe Fionn would have done that, he loved Bran like his own son.'

'But Bran's not dead?' Paul asked.

'Oh no, just sleeping, like a lot of the heroes of old, he's just sleeping.'

'And he's still sleeping?'

Criogar's feelers brushed Paul's cheeks as if he were nodding. 'He's still sleeping.'

'But what happened to Fionn?' Paul asked then.

The image of the warrior and the fairy woman standing on the water faded and was replaced by the glowing red-black coals again — but only for a moment, and then these too faded. The scene shifted and changed and Paul found he was standing at the foot of tall black cliffs on a rough stony beach. Behind him the sea pounded against the stones and the boy could almost smell the sharp salt air, and feel the dampness on his cheeks and in his hair.

'Where are we?' he asked, looking out. Stretching along as far as he could see on either side was a long line of dark cliffs. There was no sign of any buildings or any other people.

'Krik-it, krik-it, I cannot say,' Criogar whispered harshly. 'Look,' he commanded.

The boy with the cricket on his shoulder moved slowly down the beach, walking carefully over the smooth, slippery stones. Criogar led Paul up to what looked like a sheer smooth wall, but when the boy got up close beside it he found there was a small opening in the stone. He stooped down and peered in, and then wrinkled his nose. It smelt of seaweed, dead fish and damp rot.

'Go inside,' Criogar whispered.

'Must I?' Paul asked.

'If you wish to find out what happened to Fionn, you must,' the cricket said.

Paul squeezed through the little opening in the stone and found he was in a small corridor. It was very low and dark, but Criogar said something in his own language and then the walls began to glow softly with a pale green light. The corridor wound around and around, moving deeper and deeper into the cliff, and soon the booming and pounding of the waves had disappeared and the air no longer smelt of the sea. The corridor began to grow and soon Paul didn't have to walk stooped over, and then he rounded a corner — and found he was facing a door!

The door was huge, and made of a strange black-looking wood. There were bands of metal with thick studs set into it, and these were covered with green rust. There seemed to be no lock or bolt on the door.

Paul stopped, looking at it in amazement. 'It looks very old,' he said at last, and his voice rustled and whispered all around him.

'It is,' Criogar rasped. 'Now, you must listen to me very carefully. Once we go inside, you must touch nothing and say nothing. Remember, touch nothing, say nothing,' he warned. 'Now, step up to the door, and lay both hands flat against the wood.'

Paul stepped up to the door and did as Criogar had commanded. The wood felt smooth and cool beneath his hands, but then it began to change. It grew warm — not hot, just warm — and the strange black wood began to glow softly golden. The warm light ran up along the metal bands and the rust fell away, revealing the smooth shining golden metal beneath.

And then the door began to open.

It opened with no sound at all — no creakings or groanings, no cracklings or rustlings. Paul hesitated for a few moments, but Criogar's antennae brushed against his cheek, and he heard the merest whisper of the cricket's voice in his ear. 'Step inside.'

Paul stepped inside.

He found he was standing in a huge circular room that stretched as far as he could see. There were tall candles set about the room, and as he watched, they puffed alight one by one, and shed a soft warm light around the room. The boy took a few steps forward and looked around. There were weapons on the walls, long spears and shining swords, short knives, battle-axes, clubs, and shields, either small and round or long and broad. There were tattered pieces of cloth also hanging on the wall which it took him a few moments to recognise as flags and banners. He walked slowly into the centre of the room; he wasn't frightened now, just curious.

The first thing he noticed were long grooves set into the floor. The grooves were long and narrow, and looked a little like coffins — except that they were made out of some sort of glass. They were all around the room, arranged in a circle, rather like the spokes of a wheel. Paul then looked down — and jumped. He was standing on another glass panel.

He knelt on the floor and looked at it, and then he looked around again. All the other glass panels seemed to be pointing in towards this one. He leaned over and looked into it, but there was dust over the glass. Paul pulled a handkerchief from his pocket and gently rubbed it across the glass...

There was the face of a man underneath.

He fell back, his heart thumping with fright. But then he felt Criogar's antennae brush against his cheek, and he knew the cricket wouldn't let him come to any harm, so he crept forward again. He looked into the glass panel. The face was still there, but the eyes were closed and there was no movement.

Paul frowned, there was something familiar about the face. He rubbed his handkerchief across the glass again, and then moved aside so the light from one of the candles could fall on it. The face was that of a middle-aged man, with red hair and beard streaked with grey, and there were wrinkles on his forehead and at the side of his nose. Around his head there was a simple gold band, and his arms, which were crossed over his chest, also had thick gold bracelets on them. A long golden sword lay by his right-hand side and there was a tall hunting spear by his other side.

Paul recognised him then. It was Fionn! And he was not dead, because as he watched very carefully, he could see the ancient warrior's chest rising and falling ever so slowly. He wasn't dead, but only sleeping, like King Arthur in Avalon. Paul looked around at all the other glass panels set into the floor — did the rest of the Knights of the Fianna sleep here also. The cricket would know. 'Criogar...?' he began, and suddenly the cave with its flickering candles disappeared in a flash of red light.

Paul felt as if he were spinning down into a pool of red and black water, falling... falling... falling...

...and found he was staring into the black and red coals in his grandmother's fireplace. He twisted his head, but Criogar had disappeared, and only then did he remember that the cricket had told him to say nothing.

The boy sat before the dying fire for a long time, wondering whether he had dreamt it all, about Bran and the fairy woman in the lake, and Fionn, sleeping with the other Knights of the Fianna in a cave, waiting to ride out and do battle again. Had it been a dream? He stood up and yawned; he would ask his grandmother in the morning.

But Paul didn't ask his grandmother in the morning, because by that time he already knew the answer. When he had been getting undressed, his handkerchief had fallen from his pocket, and as he bent down to pick it up, he found it was thick with heavy grey dust! It had been a new handkerchief and the only time he had used it that day was when he had wiped clean the glass in that cave.

It had all been real.

The Dog, the Cat and Saint Patrick

*Have you ever noticed how intelligent some dogs and cats are?
Sometimes they seem to be almost human, and know exactly what
you are about to say and do. There is an ancient Irish tale which
tells how St Patrick was responsible for creating the most
intelligent dogs and cats in Ireland ...*

Flann Ó Duibhir was sitting on a rock, basking in the late
summer sunshine, minding his father's sheep when he first
saw the strange woman coming up the hill towards him.
The young man slipped off the warm stone and reached
for the long stick which lay by his side. Flann looked
around carefully, but there didn't seem to be anyone else
near. He turned back to the stranger; it looked as if she was
alone, but he was still very cautious. It might be a trick;
while she talked to him, thieves might steal his father's
sheep. It had happened before.

   Flann raised the stick in the air and waved it, just to show
that he was not unarmed. 'Who are you?' he shouted.
'What do you want?'

   The woman stopped and then smiled. She was a tall,
broad woman, with thick black hair and darkly suntanned
skin. Her eyes were black and seemed to glitter slightly,
and her teeth were very white. She was wearing a long
dress of a dark brown cloth that swept the ground and
was tied around her waist by a simple leather cord.

'Who are you?' Flann asked again, becoming nervous when she didn't reply. He had never seen the woman before, nor had he ever seen anyone like her. She was very beautiful.

'My name is Thana,' she said quietly.

Flann frowned. He was a young man of no more than eighteen, with long straight black hair, nut brown skin from his outdoor life and dark brown eyes. 'That's not an Irish name,' he said.

The woman smiled, showing her small white teeth again. 'My father was... a foreigner,' she said.

'Thana... Thana,' Flann said, trying to pronounce the name the same way the woman had, but it still didn't seem to sound right.

She laughed. 'Don't worry; very few people can say it properly. What's your name?' she asked.

'Flann,' he said, 'Flann Ó Duibhir. My father owns all the land around here; these are his sheep I'm minding.' He looked at the stick in his hand and lowered it. 'We have had some trouble with bandits,' he explained. 'Where do you come from?' he said then.

Thana waved her arm towards the east. 'Over there,' she said vaguely.

'From Tara?' Flann asked.

The woman shook her head. 'No, not from Tara, although I've been there.'

'What are you doing here then?' Flann said. 'This is a long way from Tara.'

Thana shrugged. She had now come so close to Flann that he was staring into her hard glittering black eyes. They were like mirrors. If he looked closely enough, he could see tiny twin reflections of himself in them. 'I'm just wandering around,' she said. She paused and then added, 'I've been watching you for a few days now.'

'Why?' Flann asked, becoming wary again. So, he had been right — someone had been watching him. He had been feeling a little strange over the past few days, and on several occasions he had turned around rather suddenly, almost expecting someone to be standing behind him.

'For no reason,' Thana said. 'You're a very handsome man, Flann,' she continued, 'you must be married by now.'

Flann shook his head. 'No, not yet, but soon,' he said. 'I'm sure my father will find me a suitable wife.'

Thana hesitated for a few minutes. She looked down at the rich, green grass and then up into the clear blue sky and finally she looked at Flann. 'Would he have me as your wife?' she asked then.

The young man took a step back in amazement. He couldn't think of anything to say, all he could do was to shake his head.

Thana smiled. 'Is that a yes or a no?' she asked.

Flann swallowed hard. 'I'm not sure,' he said. 'I don't know…' he began. 'But I don't even know you,' he said at last.

'If your father picked a wife for you, would you know her?' Thana asked, and all Flann could do was to shake his head. 'Well then, why can your father not ask my father for permission for you to marry me?'

Flann worked it out very slowly, and then he said, 'But I don't think my father would ask your father for you — I'm sure my father doesn't even know your father.'

Thana laughed then. It was a strange wild sound that sent the birds in the trees flapping and cawing up into the heavens and sent the sheep scurrying to the far side of the field. 'Your father knows mine,' she said, 'you can be sure of that.'

'But why would he…' Flann began, and the woman raised her small, long-fingered hand.

'Because I would bring a fine dowry with me,' she said.

Flann thought about that. When a girl married, she was expected to bring a dowry with her. Sometimes it was money, but more often it was land or cattle which, in Erin, was considered to be just as valuable as money. 'I suppose if it was a good dowry,' he said softly.

'I would imagine there would be a farm and at least a hundred head of fine cattle.'

Flann's eyes widened in surprise. That was a fortune! He looked at the strange woman for a few minutes and then said, 'Why?'

'Why?' she asked.

'Yes,' he said, 'why? You don't know me, you've never met me before, and now you want me to marry you. And yet you could have your pick of men. Why, with a dowry like that you could marry a prince.'

'But I don't want to marry a prince,' she said. 'I want to marry you.'

'But why?' Flann asked again.

'Because an old wise woman once told me that I would marry a shepherd boy, and she said that if I did I would live long and happily, and that my children would be remembered for generations in Erin. Is that a good enough reason?' she asked.

Flann nodded. 'That's a good enough reason,' he said.

Flann's father was very doubtful when he learned that his son had met a strange woman on the hillside and now he wanted to marry her. Or rather that she wanted to marry him. But when he heard of the huge dowry she would bring with her, he quickly said yes. Flann was his youngest son, and he was relieved to see him married into a wealthy family. Arrangements were quickly made and Flann and Thana were married barely three months later. The wedding was huge and was attended by all the lords and ladies of Erin and, if anyone thought that Thana's family were a strange, dark-looking, quiet people, no one said anything that might spoil the wedding day. So, on the following day, Flann said good-bye to his family and then he and his wife set off for her farm in the south-west of Erin.

They both worked hard there and the farm quickly grew to be one of the largest in the kingdom. A little more than a year later, Thana gave birth to a beautiful black-haired, brown-eyed boy that looked just like his father and two years after that, she gave birth to a lovely black-haired, black-eyed girl that was the very image of her mother.

The years passed and they were both very happy together, and their babies quickly grew into lovely children. And then one day a stranger came to the farm...

Duff, the boy, saw the stranger first, and for some reason he suddenly felt frightened. He was wandering along the beach below the farm, gathering up the seaweed with his sister, which would later be spread out on the ground and used as a fertiliser for the soil. It was a trick his mother had taught his father, and one of the reasons they grew the finest and strongest crops.

The boy straightened up and shaded his eyes, looking at the man walking slowly and steadily down along the beach. Without turning around, he called his sister. 'Duvessa, come here, look.'

The young girl straightened up and turned to look at her brother. 'What's the matter...' she started to say, but then she too saw the stranger. She crunched through the rough sand to his side. 'Who is it?' she said softly.

Duff shook his head. 'I don't know; but he frightens me,' he said in a whisper.

Duvessa shivered and then hugged her arms tightly around her body. 'Me too,' she said.

Although there was nearly two years between the boy and girl, they were the best of friends, and never fought nor quarrelled. Indeed, some people even thought that they were actually twins because they were so alike, both in looks and manners.

The stranger came closer, crunching solidly through the rough sand, and hard, dried sea-wrack. He was a short, dark-skinned man, with sharp grey eyes, and a big, hooked nose, and he was completely bald, except for a fringe of hair that ran right around his head in a circle. He was wearing a rough brown robe that almost reached the ground, which was belted around his waist with a white cord, and he carried a long thick stick, which he dug into the ground with every step he took. He saw the two children, waved and hurried up to them.

'Hello,' he said. His voice was soft and whispery, and he spoke Irish with a strange, whistling sort of accent. 'My name is Patrick, what's yours?'

But the boy and girl just looked at the man and said nothing.

'I have travelled from Tara,' the man said. 'I am visiting every town and village, farm and house on the road. I hope to travel all around Erin before returning to Tara. It's a very long journey,' he added. 'Are you still not going to tell me your names?' he said then.

'My mother said that there is a magic in names,' Duff said, 'and if we tell you our true names, then you will have power over us, and be able to cast spells on us.'

The small dark man looked shocked. 'But that is wrong! How can your mother tell you such things?'

'My mother isn't wrong!' Duvessa said quickly.

Patrick nodded quickly. 'No, no, of course she's not wrong; I didn't mean to say that. But look, I've told you my name, haven't I? Maybe we could swap names?'

But Duff and Duvessa both shook their heads firmly. 'No!'

Patrick looked a little surprised as if he didn't know what to do. At last he said, 'Well, will you take me to see your father or mother?'

The young boy and girl thought about it for a few moments before they nodded silently. And then they both turned around and headed back up the beach.

Patrick followed on behind them, his hard-soled sandals crunching and rattling along the sand and stones. The two children were the strangest he had ever met since he had returned to the land of Erin. He looked closely at them, but they didn't seem to be fairy-children; they didn't have the long faces, pointed chins, nose and sharp ears, and their eyes were the proper shape. They were very dark though and, although he could see that there was at least two years between them, they looked almost like twins. There is something amiss here, he thought.

The two children met their father at the far end of the beach. He had seen the stranger approach and had grabbed his spear and strapped on his sword and then hurried down to meet them. These were dangerous times, with bandits roaming the land and pirates sailing the seas, and he didn't want his children to come to any harm. Duff and Duvessa ran to their father as soon as they saw him.

'A stranger,' Duff said, 'he comes from Tara. He says he's visiting every town and village in Erin.'

'And he said his name is Patrick,' Duvessa added. 'I've never heard a name like that, have you?' she asked her father.

Flann looked sharply at the small, dark man with the bright grey eyes. 'I've heard the name before,' he said quietly, both answering his daughter and speaking to the stranger.

The small man nodded. 'I am that Patrick,' he said, 'the one you have heard about.'

Flann lowered his spear and smiled. 'I've heard a lot about you,' he said. 'These are my children, Duff and Duvessa.'

Patrick smiled slightly. 'I don't think they wanted me to know their names,' he said.

Flann nodded. 'That would be their mother's doing. She has some very strange, old-fashioned ideas.' He knelt down beside the boy and girl. 'Now, why don't you run on home and tell your mother that we will be having a guest for our evening meal.'

'Who is he?' Duvessa whispered to her father.

'That is Patrick, the Holy Man,' he said. 'People are already beginning to call him a saint.'

The girl looked over at the man in the rough clothes. 'He frightens me,' she said, and then she and her brother turned and ran off in the direction of their father's farm.

Flann and Patrick stood and watched them until they had disappeared over a hill. 'They are fine children,' Patrick said.

'Aye,' Flann nodded, 'any father would be proud of them.'

'Their names are very unusual,' Patrick said.

Flann nodded again. 'My wife, Thana, picked them. They mean "black" and "little black beauty".'

Patrick shook his head again and his eyes looked troubled. 'Strange names indeed. And you say that your wife's name is Thana?'

'I had never heard of it myself before I met her,' Flann said.

'Thana... Thana... Thana,' Patrick said slowly. 'Perhaps it is short for something,' he said.

Flann began to shake his head and then stopped. 'The only time I ever heard my wife called by any other name was at our wedding when her father was speaking quietly to her in a corner, and he called her "Chaorthanach". I thought it might be his pet name for her — you know, the way some fathers have special names for their favourite children. I sometimes call Duvessa, "Vessy", but her mother doesn't like it.'

'Chaorthanach,' Patrick said the word slowly, dragging it out. 'Chaor-than-ach.' He had turned pale beneath his dark tan.

'Have you heard that name before?' Flann asked when he saw the strange look on the man's face.

Patrick nodded. 'I've heard of it,' he said softly, so softly that Flann had to strain to hear him.

'What's wrong?' he asked.

Patrick shook his head. 'I don't know yet. I'll have to meet your wife to see...'

'To see what?'

'I'm not sure. Tell me,' he said then, 'how did you meet your wife...?'

And as they walked across the dunes towards the farm, Flann told him the strange tale of his meeting with Thana, and how he came to marry her.

Thana was waiting at the door for the two men. She was dressed in her finest clothes and had brushed her coal-black hair until it shone almost purple. Duff and Duvessa had been sent off to bed to keep them out of the way.

Flann walked over and put his arm around his wife's shoulders. 'This is Thana,' he said proudly.

Patrick bowed. 'My lady,' he said politely.

Thana bowed her head slightly. 'You are welcome here to my home,' she said properly. 'You will eat and rest with us?' she asked.

'I will be honoured to,' Patrick said quietly. He hadn't expected to be turned away. The Irish people at that time were famous for their hospitality and travellers were always welcome at their doors. Indeed, it was considered to be a great insult if someone refused to pass the night at a house where they had been invited to stay.

'Then you are welcome,' Thana said, although Patrick didn't think that she meant it.

The two men ate alone and, while they were eating, Patrick told Flann how he had been captured by pirates as a child and sold into slavery in Ireland. He told how, while he had been herding wild pigs on Slieve Mish, he had seen a vision of an angel, who had shown him how to escape. Then Patrick told how he had returned home to his own land to train to be a priest in the church of Christ, and how he eventually returned to the land of Erin to bring the Word of God to the pagans there.

Flann had already heard a little about the holy man. Indeed, all Erin had heard about the stranger who had lit a fire on Slane at the Time of Darkness, when no fire was supposed to be lit before the Arch Druid and the High King lit their own fire at Tara. Flann had also heard how the small, dark man had defeated Lucemael, the Arch Druid, in a magic battle that had brought darkness and snow down over Tara's walls in the middle of a summer's day.

When Patrick had finished speaking and explaining about the new religion that was springing up all across Europe, he sat back and waited. He could see that Flann was interested. 'Well?' he asked at last.

Flann nodded. 'Yes; it makes sense. But you will have to tell me more about this new god... and you must tell my wife and the children also. Duff and Duvessa are already in bed, but you can speak to Thana now. I'll call her.' He stood up to go into the other room and call his wife, but she suddenly appeared in the doorway, wearing her long, heavy cloak. 'Oh.' Flann stopped. 'I was going to ask you to come and listen to the holy man...' he began.

'I have no wish to listen to any holy man,' Thana snapped, her face set in a dark and angry frown. 'Nor do I want to hear about his god. I have my own gods, and they are more powerful than his!' She spun around, her cloak billowing out behind her and her footsteps echoed on the stone floors as she hurried out into the night.

Flann came back with a strange look on his face. 'I have never seen her like that before,' he said in a whisper. 'I can't think what has upset her so.'

'You have never seen her like this before?' Patrick asked.

Flann shook his head. 'No, never. I've seen her angry and annoyed. But I've never seen her in such a terrible rage.'

The holy man stood up and walked to the fire. He stood staring into the dancing flames for a few moments before turning around and facing the man. 'I think you should sit down,' he said quietly. 'I have something to tell you, something shocking.'

'What is it?'

Patrick shook his head. 'Sit down first,' he said.

Flann looked at him for a moment, and then he obediently sat down on the wooden stool. 'Well?' he demanded.

Patrick looked at him for long moments, his hands folded into his long sleeves, his head bowed. With the red firelight behind him, he looked almost frightening.

'Well?' Flann asked again.

'I have met your wife before,' Patrick said very softly. 'She knows me, and that is why she does not like me, nor my god. We have fought before, and on both occasions I won.'

'Fought? Fought?' Flann asked. 'How could you have fought with my wife?'

'Because you wife is not a real woman,' Patrick said. 'She is An Chaorthanach.'

Flann continued staring at him, not saying anything.

'And An Chaorthanach means the Devil's Mother. Your wife is the Devil's Mother!'

'No!' Flann shook his head, 'You're playing a joke... she can't be.'

Patrick suddenly turned and pointed towards the door. 'What are you?' he shouted in a strong, commanding voice.

Thana stepped into the room. She had crept back after allowing her husband and the holy man to think that she had gone out for a walk. She tried to speak, to tell her husband some lie, but the words got stuck in her throat and she suddenly heard herself telling the truth. 'I am An Chaorthanach.'

'Why did you marry me?' Flann asked miserably, 'Why?'

The creature shook her head, but Patrick said, 'Tell him.'

'Because I wanted to have human children,' she said. 'I can only stay on the world for a short length of time, but I wanted to have children of my own that would do my evil work for me.' Thana tried to hold her two hands across her mouth to stop herself from telling everything, but the holy man was too powerful for her.

Flann turned to Patrick. 'What can I do?' he whispered.

The saint shrugged. 'I can send her back to Hell, if you wish.'

The man nodded.

Patrick then made the Sign of the Cross in front of the woman, and suddenly her shape began to change. At first it was as if a thin fog had come down over her face, and then the fog thickened and now it crept slowly down her body. When she was completely covered with this thick fog, it began to change colour, turning from a grey-white to an ugly blue-black. Red and gold sparks spun and danced within this fog, and thin streamers of fire shot out and crackled on the stone floor. And then the fog began to shrink in on itself. Sounds came from it now. They were almost human, but towards the end they sounded like the snuffling and grunting of a pig — and Flann was glad that he couldn't see what was happening within the fog. When it had shrunk to a ball no bigger than a man's head, it suddenly spun around very quickly, and then shot out through the window and disappeared into the night sky with a thin, high-pitched tearing sound.

'She's gone,' Patrick said softly.

'And what about my children?' Flann asked, in a tight voice.

The holy man shook his head sadly. 'They are also the children of the Devil's Mother,' he reminded him. 'In a way that would make them almost a half-brother and half-sister to the Devil himself.'

'But what can we do?' Flann asked. 'I won't allow you to kill them,' he said.

'But if they continue to live they will grow up to be evil and will bring much sorrow into this world.'

'Can you change them then?' Flann asked. 'Can you change them into something else, like you did with... with my wife.'

'I only returned your wife to her true form,' Patrick said, 'But yes, I could change them.'

'Change them then,' Flann said. 'Change them so that they cannot do any evil.'

'What will I change them into?' the holy man asked.

'I don't know. Anything — a dog or a cat even. That way they could stay here and I would still be able to look after them.'

Patrick nodded. 'As you wish then.'

Flann led Patrick to the children's bedroom, and carefully eased open the heavy wooden door. They were both asleep beneath heavy woollen blankets and fur coverings. They looked so peaceful and innocent that Flann turned to the holy man. 'Are you sure they will grow up to be evil?' he asked.

Patrick nodded his head. 'Duff will become a great warrior and will eventually lead the country into a terrible war which will kill many thousands of soldiers, and leave a huge part of the countryside laid waste.'

'And Duvessa?'

'Duvessa will grow up to a beautiful young woman, and she will marry the king of the land of the Britons. Then she will kill him and rule the country in his place. But his brothers will gather up their own armies and there will be a terrible civil war.'

'And if they both grow up that will happen?' Flann asked.

Patrick nodded. 'I was told this in a vision.'

'Then do what you have to do.'

But all the holy man did was to walk into the centre of the room and raise both hands high and speak in his own Latin language. He prayed for a few moments like this and then he slowly crossed himself, and stepped back to the door.

Flann was just about to ask him when he was going to work his magic when he noticed that the coverings on the beds were shifting and moving, and even as he watched he saw that they were falling, until there were only two small lumps near the head of the bed. And then these covers twitched and two small furry heads peeked out over the covers. One barked and one mewed.

Patrick had changed Duff into a black dog and Duvessa into a black cat!

Of course, there are some animals that are very human indeed, especially dogs and cats that are completely black. And is it not strange that there are a lot of superstitions attached to black cats and dogs?